To my Super Six who I love very much;-

Isaac
Jacob
Isabella
Jade
Ella (aka The Fig) or is it The Fig (aka Ella)?
Emelia (aka The Pumpkin) or is it The Pumpkin (aka
Emelia)?

Part One

Becoming A Golf Club Manager
And
Writing This Book

Chapter One

Golf

On reflection, I ought to have got to the game of golf sooner than I did. My maternal grandfather had once played the game at a high level, I lived in a town with two municipal golf courses and my father had some old clubs gathering dust in the corner of the outhouse in the garden.

I had participated in a number of sports before turning to golf. Of course, football was a regular, but I also had a bash at cricket, rugby, swimming, stoolball, tennis, track and field events, basketball and hockey through school. There was also an element of a misspent youth with snooker and pool, a dabble at darts and even a bash at boxing (but not for long!).

So it was the summer of 1974, aged 15, when my cousin and I decided we would have a try at golf. We gathered up as much equipment as we could, made sandwiches for lunch, tied our plimsolls to the golf bag and then caught the No.43 bus to make our way to the golf course.

On arrival, we paid our green fee and off we went. I remember little about the actual day other than we were clearly not put off and continued to play although on an occasional basis.

In December 1974, my grandfather's former golf buddy passed away and his widow wanted me to have his clubs and I, obviously, very gratefully accepted them. At that time of year, the weather is not particularly conducive to golf (almost half a century later, I'm still not a keen winter golfer!) and I remember going stir crazy at being unable to use my new clubs out on the course. When everyone was out at home, I'd get them out to have a practice swing. That is until the eight iron took a divot out of the twenty six foot long lounge carpet!! Mother was not amused. Father even less so!

Notwithstanding that event, I was allowed to continue with my interest in golf albeit, it was stressed that it would be an outdoor pursuit from that moment. We lived in a block of six terraced houses and at the far end lived the retiring Captain of one of those two clubs and he smoothed the way to my cousin and I joining the club in March 1975.

Up until August of that year, we played regularly with what was then a thriving junior section at the club. During that month, my Aunt and Uncle took my cousin and I to Scotland for a holiday and of course, we were allowed to take our clubs. In the ten days that we were there, I think we played every day and I certainly remember playing both courses in Ayr (Belleisle and Seafield) as well as Girvan, Stranraer, Portpatrick, Troon, Prestwick and Turnberry. Turnberry remains a favourite golfing destination as a result of that visit. I can still remember standing at the bottom of the steps that lead to the hotel and us not daring to venture up them! How times subsequently changed when I took my family to Troon for the Open Championship in 2004 and having camped for the week, we stayed a night in the hotel, my sons (aged 9 and 8 at the time) and I played the course and my daughter, aged 7, played the piano in the Turnberry Restaurant.

We returned home on a Thursday and the following Monday saw us play in our first junior competition. In those days, juniors were automatically allocated a handicap of 36 on joining and clearly the experience we had had in Scotland benefitted us greatly. I was round in 84 strokes for a net 48 to finish second to my cousin who beat me by three strokes!

Our handicaps were very quickly slashed by twelve strokes which meant that we were not eligible to play in the men's competitions. We entered the medal the following Saturday and I went round in 83 for a net 59 which further reduced my handicap to 19 and by the end of August 1975, I was playing off 13!

Further progress was made and I eventually reached a single figure handicap and whilst some cups and trophies had been won along the way, my greatest achievement was in reaching the semi final of the inaugural Club Championship. In fact, it is also probably one of my greatest disappointments as, with being three up with three holes to play, I went on to lose on the second play off hole. I should have reached the final.

I continued to enjoy the game until the early 1980's when marriage and domesticity took over. I returned to play in the mid-eighties, but relocation to London with work in 1988 reduced my golf to the very occasional round.

It would be some fifteen years before I played regularly again although that was on the back of my two sons taking an interest in the game after having had a go at most other sports.

Following this rejuvenation, and after starting to work in golf club management, I now find that my enthusiasm to play is not the same. I'm not sure that this is a result of the skill level of my sons making my game look so inferior or whether it's because having been at a golf club all week, the desire to return and play at the weekend is not great.

I do know that each time I do play, I walk off having thoroughly enjoyed it but then it could be months before I play again.

Chapter Two

Work

Even though I believe I have a reasonable level of intelligence, deciding to go to university was never really an option for me. In those days, it was really only the brightest that went and I don't think I was in that category.

Maths was always my subject at school and I thought I would head in that direction. In hindsight, I should have gone down the Accountancy route but I didn't.

I applied for two jobs – one with the Civil Service and one with a bank. Perhaps a fair recollection of the job market in 1975, I was offered both positions! However, as the Civil Service role was in their artificial limb department, I had no hesitation in accepting the position in the bank.

In the previous chapter, I mentioned the holiday in Scotland with my cousin and on our return on the Thursday, the appointment letter from the bank was waiting for me – to start on the following Monday. This prompted a hasty shopping trip the following day with mother to buy a suit, shirt etc.

My first day coincided with that first junior competition and therefore I had to go in and ask if I could leave early so that my father could pick me up and drop me off at the course after work. The early finish was agreed and I can only assume that suitable arrangements for pick up had been made as there were no mobile telephones in those days. In fact, I'm not necessarily convinced we had a landline at that point.

I spent five years working as a cashier and in clerical duties before my first promotion which was handling bulk coin, hence the reason why I was promoted and not one of the forty two girls that were ahead of me in the queue.

Although I didn't go to university, I was keen to continue studying and by the time promotion came along, I had already passed the Ordinary National Certificate in Business Studies and had made a start on the banking examinations.

I rose through the ranks in branches, spent two years on the recruitment and training side before being appointed Manager of Personal Business of a large branch. However, less than a year down the line, the bank asked me to move south to become a Bank Manager in my own right at the age of twenty nine which I obviously accepted.

After five years in the London area and having completed my banking exams, I moved back home having been appointed Bank Manager of the biggest branch in the network at that time. During my time there, the bank made the decision to include providing financial services into the role of the Bank Manager. This meant further studying and the Financial Planning Certificate was passed.

When the opportunity to leave came along, I took it and joined a neighbour who had his own Independent Financial Advisory practice, spent two years with him before taking over the business lock, stock and barrel following his decision to withdraw. Although all types of financial advice was offered, the majority of business was mortgage based, hence the successful completion of the Certificate of Mortgage Advice Practice – my qualification cup is full to the brim!!

As I said above, the business was largely mortgage based and I remembered being out in the car visiting a client one day when I heard on the radio that Northern Rock had announced that they would start offering mortgages at five times salary and knew then that the bottom was going to drop out of the market and soon! I wasn't wrong.

By this time, I was spending a lot of time in golf clubs with my play and more frequently, with my sons. In 2006, we had joined Radcliffe on Trent Golf Club and that was the first club I had been a member of that had a full time paid Secretary/Manager and the more I saw of what his role entailed, the more I saw that there was a potential opening for me and perhaps a new career path.

Chapter Three

Golf Becomes Work

Having joined Radcliffe on Trent Golf Club, there were many more opportunities for my sons to play in competitions and matches, and I was generally there in attendance when they were playing.

When the organiser of the Junior Section decided that he no longer wanted to continue in the role and I suppose I was the obvious person to ask to replace him and I agreed.

A part of this role was to sit on their Match & Handicaps Committee and this allowed me to start seeing the workings of the golf club and more specifically, the role of the Secretary/Manager. The more I saw, the more I was convinced that I could rely on the experiences at the bank and working for myself to be successful – people management, financial management, administration, organisational and time management skills etc.

I asked if I could spend some time in the office on a work experience basis in order to gain more experience in that environment but unfortunately was declined. Though I understand that they may have seen confidentiality as an issue, they ought to have seen that as a Bank Manager and Financial Adviser, confidentiality was ingrained in me.

Undeterred, I began to apply for jobs in the golf industry but whilst I was successful in obtaining interviews, I was unsuccessful in progressing beyond that first stage of the recruitment process. The main obstacle to overcome was experience. Despite asking me for interview, this was the constant feedback I received – perhaps just a convenient excuse?

Two things happened as a result of continually being declined for the roles that I had applied for.

Firstly, I began to state in my covering letters that whilst I accepted that I didn't have any experience in the golf industry, I considered that as much as an asset as it could be interpreted as a liability. Being new would allow me to look at things with a fresh pair of eyes and from a different perspective, rather than being shackled by the past and out dated work practices. I continued my run of form of getting interviews but not much further.

Secondly, I enrolled on the Golf Club Managers' Association' Principles of Golf Club Management Training Course. I obviously had to meet the cost (£600.00) of the course myself but attended in May 2008 at the Beachlands Hotel in Weston-super-Mare. The course lasted four days and contained twenty-two different lectures covering every aspect involved in the running of a golf club. Although they were long gruelling days, that didn't stop me from being up at first light to play a few holes on the course across the road.

My progress continued in much the same vein despite the two measures detailed above! Even when the job came up at Radcliffe on Trent Golf Club later that year, I was unable to progress beyond the first interview although they had seen me in action at first hand in the Junior Organiser role and as a part of their Match & Handicaps Committee.

Once into 2009, I decided that if I hadn't been successful in getting a job by the halfway mark, I would have no alternative but to give it up as an unfulfilled dream.

I decided that to give it one last push, I would go into the office of a couple of clubs to get the experience that potential employers so desired. Whereas my own club had declined to give me that opportunity, I was very grateful that Notts (Hollinwell) and Rushcliffe allowed me to do that and I spent a week in each.

Now I'm not saying I learnt everything I needed to know in those two weeks, and in fact, some of the time was spent completing mundane tasks like addressing and stamping envelopes but nevertheless, I now had some valuable work experience to add to my Curriculum Vitae – and it worked!!

Both of my next two application saw me progress to a second interview. In relation to the first job, I narrowly missed out on the position but in relation to the latter, I was offered the position, which of course, I very gladly accepted.

At the second interview for the job that I had been offered, I had stated that I had three objectives in terms of a career in golf club management;-

    1) Get a job!
    2) Be nominated for the Golf Club Manager of the Year competition within five years of my appointment and
    3) Manage an Open Championship venue before I retire.

I was now on the way – with my first objective completed.

Chapter Fore!

This Book

Now I have to be honest here, when I set out to write this introductory part of the book, I had no intention of writing a fourth chapter. However, I couldn't resist the opportunity of having a 'Chapter Fore!'

(Editor's Note – For those that are unfamiliar with golfing terms, when golfers hit an errant ball that may be heading for other players, they should shout 'Fore!' so that they may take some defensive action).

There are so many things happen at a golf club that I have often said that I would include it when I get around to writing my memoirs, and as I approach my tenth anniversary in the role, I thought that now is the time to get on with it.

On hearing that I am a Golf Club Manager, many people think that it's a 'cushy number' and all you do is either talk golf all day, play golf all day or watch people talk and play golf all day. Nothing could be further from the truth! In fact, there are probably more days that go by that have absolutely nothing to do with golf whatsoever (hence the title of the book!).

A golf club is a medium sized business these days and all the usual issues that affect other types of business apply.

ENJOY!

Part Two

The Diary
Of A
Golf Club Manager

Chapter 1

Lingdale Golf Club
Woodhouse Eaves, Leicestershire

Managing Secretary

1st June 2009 – 30th May 2014

Lingdale Golf Club

Many golf clubs were formed either in the latter part of the 19th century or the early part of the 20th century as the game of golf developed or in the early 1990's when, following a report by the Royal & Ancient Golf Club of St Andrews published a report saying that the demand would be greater, farmers decided to either develop their land for golf or sold their land off for golf. Lingdale Golf Club was formed as a nine hole course in 1967 in between these dates.

In 1966, Course Architect David Tucker purchased sixty acres of land in the Charnwood Forest area and the following year, the course opened. Shortly after, it was sold to the Brush Engineering Company of Loughborough. They used it as their social club and continued to develop the golf course.

In 1982, the members of Lingdale purchased the club and by the end of that decade, the course had been extended to eighteen holes following acquisition of more land situated on the other side of Joe Moores Lane.

Development of the course and club followed quickly after when the greens were renewed and constructed to USGA specification and a new clubhouse and professional's shop was built.

In 2017, the club celebrated their 50th Anniversary with a number of special celebrations that included playing the original nine holes, a gala dinner, an Anniversary Weekend competition and a special Open Competition.

Monday 1st June 2009

My first official day in post! I say official as I did do a few days prior as an acclimatisation exercise. I also came in yesterday with my eldest son in order to re-configure the office furniture!!

And that's when I made my first mistake – a day before I officially started! To move some of the desks around, we had to temporarily turn off the desktop computer and then switch it back on once the furniture had been re-arranged. Little did I know that a competition was underway and that the computer switch off meant that competitors could not record their scores directly into the system and as a result, they had to be manually input the day after. Oops!!

When I called in March to hand deliver my application for the position, my predecessor had the desks facing the wall and therefore couldn't see what was going on or who was coming in and out of the club!! I wanted to see more and be seen more than that.

I'm sharing the office with a lady who is slightly older than me but is well entrenched into the role and the club. She been working here for a number of years, and following the departure of various managers before me, she's been left to hold the fort until the new man takes up the reins and this time, that new man is me!

Not only that but her husband, who died a few years previously had been the Captain of the club and she herself plays the game!

Tuesday 2nd June 2009

My first piece of correspondence to deal with – a travel expense claim from one of the unsuccessful candidates for the position - how cheeky!

There was never any indication that travel expenses would be paid and I established that he didn't make any such enquiries when he had arrived for either of his two interviews.

A polite decline to his request was sent.

I hadn't warmed to this guy previously as I had come across him on two other occasions. He was the current incumbent at the club where I had my first interview (he was moving on to a new club) and then a few months later, I met him at a club in Sussex. We had both applied and been successful in obtaining an interview for their vacancy.

As an aside and in relation to the latter, the club did contact me subsequent to the interview to ask where they would pay my expenses and I told them to donate them to their junior section.

Monday 8th June 2009

Over the weekend, the postman has been and brought a letter from Environmental Health – there are issues with our Reed Bed that acts as our sewerage system. A reed bed is an aquatic plant based system that allows bacteria, fungi and algae to digest the sewage and clean the water.

For some reason, they have been monitoring the quality of the final water and it's not meeting the standards expected and required.

As a result, I learn that reed beds are so yesterday in being an effective sewerage treatment mechanism and it becomes clear that an alternative method will be required.

Monday 22nd June 2009

Big night tonight – my first meeting of the Management Committee!

The meeting was ok but my view on why they are there has changed. Whilst I thought that their role was to drive the club forward into the future, and there are a few members that want to do that, it became clear to me that the majority are only there to either;-

- a) Have the kudos of being on the Committee or
- b) Look after the interests of their golfing buddies or
- c) Look after their own interests.

I thought that when they walked into the room for their meeting, all of their personal views went out of the window and it was club, club and club. Unfortunately, I was wrong!

Sunday 18th October 2009

I'm in work today to oversee my first County competition, the Mixed Baxter Trophy. I'd always felt that when the club has such visitors, then I should be there in attendance in case of need.

As it happens, nothing out of the ordinary presented itself on the day and everything went smoothly.

Saturday 14th November 2009

Today was memorable for two things.

Firstly, in the afternoon, I had attended the Annual General Meeting of the English Schools' Golf Association and had been nominated for, and subsequently elected to the position of Assistant Secretary.

Secondly, in the evening, I had been invited by the Captain of the day, to be his guest speaker at the Annual Dinner Dance – he had forgotten to arrange one so asked me to speak about my first few months in the role.

Obviously I accepted but rather than providing my talk in speech form, I did it as a humorous poem which was very well received.

Friday 11th December 2009

My first Christmas Open!

Over one hundred competitors I've signed up to play in this event with a shotgun start at 10.30am. (A shotgun start means that everyone starts playing at the same time from different points around the golf course with the benefit that they all, more or less, finish playing at the same time). A two Christmas lunch and then the prize presentation for the winners follow golf.

Of course, the clubhouse is already trimmed up for the festive period and Christmas songs and carols are played to add to the feel of the day.

It's a wonderful day and all goes to plan.

Friday 1st January 2010

Although it's a Bank Holiday, I'm at work today because the new Captain takes over and there's plenty to do. As well as changing the photographs on display in the clubhouse and on the website, the incoming Captain will have provided a message that also needs to be posted on the website.

In addition, there are checks to be made to ensure that everything is on top line for the Captain's Drive In later on that day which is preceded by a New Year's luncheon.

This Drive-In tradition can best be described as golf in fancy dress! It will involve the Captain and Captain of the Ladies section being led to the first tee by a piper, in some sort of fancy dress, the theme of which they will have decided between themselves prior to the event. The theme could be something specific to them or something for the year.

Once at the first tee, the Captain and Captain of the Ladies section will each have three attempts at their drive in. The first would usually involved a hugely oversized golf club, the second using an 'exploding' golf ball and then the third with their own club and ball. Once they have both played, someone will be down the fairway and will measure the distance between the two balls, and the member that have guessed closest to that distance will win a small prize. Members will have had the opportunity to have a guess, at a cost of £1.00, before the drive in started.

After this ceremony, the newly installed Captain makes a speech and announces what his charity for the year will be. This is usually followed with a prize draw from the Professional although the timing can depend on the New Year's football fixture list, where his team are playing and what time kick off is.

Wednesday 10th February 2010

As can be the case in February, it's a bitterly cold day with temperatures near freezing and the roads around the golf club are only just passable.

This lunchtime, we're hosting a 'Women in Business Network' lunch followed by a meeting. They had a number of similar events booked with us on a monthly basis.

The Caterer has completed lunch and as staff are tidying up and the ladies have commenced their meeting, he leaves for the day but not before he is warned about the state of the roads.

Unfortunately, he doesn't heed that warning and on taking the left hand dog leg of the golf club drive, slides across the road and puts his very expensive Audi into the ditch!

Fortunately, he's ok, other than hurt with embarrassment, following his climb out of the car via the passenger door.

He claims to have been being very careful but he wasn't known for being a slow driver! His attempt to get out of the cub quick cost him two hours while waiting for the breakdown truck and thousands of pounds in repairing his car,

Wednesday 3rd March 2010

The Captain's of 2009 had decided not to nominate an external charity as their beneficiary for the year, but instead had decided to adopt a 'charity begins at home' philosophy. The funds raised would be used to buy a defibrillator, which would be sited at the club in case of need.

Today, a representative from the supplier was bringing the newly purchased machine along and providing training for the staff from the course, office and bar.

We all gathered in the foyer to receive the training when the supplier's representative said "Hello Terry"! It was none other than Les Bradd, better known as the record goalscorer of Notts County. I had known Les when we were both members of Radcliffe on Trent Golf Club and had played a few games together.

I had completely failed to recognise him!

Wednesday 5ᵗʰ May 2010

In the lead up to 1ˢᵗ January and the compilation of the 2010 Club Diary, there was one fixture that caught my attention, and imagination, that I really wanted to play in and it was played today.

The fixture is a match against a nine hole course just up the road and dates back to when this club was also a nine hole course. The format is that half of the two teams will play nine holes at one course while the other half of the two teams play at the other course. At the end of those nine holes, all the players then get in their cars, drive to the course that haven't played and then play the second nine holes. Once the match is completed, there is a dinner which is provided by each club in alternate years.

The match is referred to as 'Neither Here Nor There'.

Play is in pairs and my partner and I started at the other course before returning to our home club. Scores were fairly tight over the first few holes but then one of our opponents went to pieces when he realised that he was playing against my partner who was Bobby Roberts, a former professional footballer will Leicester City. With him being a lifelong fan and playing against one of his boyhood heroes, he just couldn't get his mind right and we ran out comfortable winners.

Monday 10th May 2010

Like most golf clubs, we have a Suggestion Book in the lounge for members to offer suggestions and comments for possible action by either myself and/or the Management Committee. My job is to review it on a regular basis, make a suitable response or bring it to the Management Committee's attention when next they meet for their consideration.

There is an 'interesting' message in it when I review it this morning;-

"Would the club consider installing a condom machine in the gents toilet"

The suggestion had been made anonymously!

The greatest thing I considered was my response which finally turned out to be;-

"The club will not be installing a condom machine in the gents toilet. However, we would suggest that you consider whether you have joined the right sort of club!!"

I did bring it to the attention of the Management Committee when they next met and they fully endorsed my response.

Wednesday 16th June 2010

On leaving the kitchen after a meeting with the Caterer, two senior members are standing at the bar having a drink. They've clearly been to a funeral judging by their sombre attire.

This is confirmed during our conversation and said that it was a former work colleague that had passed away.

There had been a small problem though – they had attended the wrong funeral!

There are two chapels at the local crematorium and there was two funerals being conducted at the same time and they had followed the wrong cortege!

Monday 16th August 2010

On arrival at the golf club this morning, the Greens Staff inform me that we have had a flagstick, together with flag, stolen from the 11th green.

Whilst it's annoying, we have become used to such petty crime/vandalism, and have spares of both to get us back to a full compliment.

Later that morning, I receive a telephone call from the local police station to say that they have had a flagstick and flag handed in to them and ask if someone from the club could call around to collect it. I tell them that I would be around shortly.

When I arrive, I explain who I am, where I am from and why I am there i.e. as a result of their earlier telephone call.

Before releasing them, they ask for identification!! Nothing had been said to me about producing identification when they called and I'd not given it a thought and had nothing on me.

After a little thought, I realised that I was wearing my club tie and on it, was the club logo that was also on the 'stolen' flag. This was sufficient to have the items returned to me.

Friday 10th December 2010

It's Christmas Open day but unfortunately, it's an easy decision to cancel following a few days of foul weather which make the golf course practically unplayable and travelling conditions for those playing are not ideal.

It has been re-arranged for 16th December.

Thursday 16th December 2010

Our plan to host the Christmas Day has been thwarted due to the continued poor weather. Again, it's an easy decision and competitors are advised in plenty of time.

We decide to give up trying to play it around this period and have a go at playing it in the spring.

Saturday 1st January 2011

A New Year and the Captain's Drive In takes place and goes to schedule.

Tuesday 18th January 2011

This evening, I attended a Children in Golf seminar.

Wednesday 19th January 2011

I receive a telephone call from a girl representing 21st Century Legacy – an organisation trying to increase the self-awareness and self-responsibility of students to unlock and maximise their potential.

They had identified us as a possible centre for the hosting of workshops for their trainers in view of our location and close proximity to the motorway network.

It became clear that we had the capacity to provide the required facilities and therefore the conversation was developed further. It was during this stage that the girl mentioned that 21st Century Legacy was headed by Dr David Hemery CBE – yes that David Hemery, the one that won the gold medal at the 1968 Olympic Games in Mexico City for the 400m hurdles!

I asked the girl to pass on my belated congratulations when she next saw him and she said that he was sat next to her and she would pass the phone over to him so I could congratulate him personally!

A brief conversation ensued and two bookings were made for the following month, both of which were attended by the man himself. Of course, we didn't let the photo opportunity pass us by!

Wednesday 2nd February 2011

It's Day Two of a Customer Service Workshop at the home of England Golf in Woodhall Spa.

The first speaker on was to talk about dress codes in clubhouses and how it was another barrier that golf puts up to stop trade and he had the temerity to wear denims while he did it!

Gasps of shock and horror!

I've always been an advocate that dress codes should be relaxed in clubhouses (not on the golf course!). I long recognised that we're in the leisure industry and therefore we ought to treat the clubhouse as such.

In my teens, jeans were work clothes made by Levi and Wrangler but during the intervening period, they have become a designer dress item made by all the main fashion houses – and their prices reflect that!

Before this workshop I had an example where two male members where stood at the office door. One was dressed in jeans, cashmere sweater and tee shirt underneath. The other in a scruffy golf top with trousers to match. The fact was that we would let the latter in as he was dressed in accordance with the dress code whereas, we shouldn't have let the former in because he didn't!

This can't be right? This has got to change!

Friday 11th March 2011

It really does seem weird in trimming up the clubhouse and playing Christmas music in March to host the twice postponed Christmas Open but it does go ahead as planned.

The vast majority that signed up to play on the original date in December played and any empty places were easily filled and as is customary, a two course Christmas lunch follows the golf.

Thursday 17th March 2011

I've been here now for almost two years and despite the fact that the clubhouse was newly built in 2006, we have a regular problem with one of the Gents toilets – it keeps getting blocked.

I've lost count of the number of Mondays I've arrived at the club after being away over the weekend and found notices on the door to say it's 'Out of Order' and I daren't tally up how much it has cost us to call out plumbers to resolve the matter. Each one that has been has solved it but none have offered any permanent solution to the problem (maybe it's not in their best interest to do so?!).

I decided today that I'd have a go at solving it myself.

As we don't have a plunger, I've rolled my sleeve up, wrapped toilet tissue around my hand and then, while pushing down on the 'material' causing the blockage, flushed the toilet!

And it worked!!

Of course, this procedure necessitates a thorough scrub afterwards but the time and money saved in the future will be vast!

Memo to self: Buy a plunger or at least some marigolds!

Wednesday 6th April 2011

If you recall from the outset of my career, I stated that I had three objectives and today, the second has been achieved.

I'm at The Kendleshire Golf Club, near Bristol and it's the Annual General Meeting of the Golf Club Manager's Association (GCMA). Once the meeting has been concluded, there will be the announcement of the Golf Club Manager of the Year award for 2010 and I'm on the shortlist of six candidates for the award.

I was perhaps a little fortunate in that the Chairman of the Management Committee at the time had also been on the selection panel that recruited me for the position. As he had also previously been the Secretary of a golf club, he was on the distribution list for the monthly magazine and a copy had advertised the forthcoming Golf Club Manager of the Year award and how candidates should be nominated.

Remembering my objective, he sent a message out to all members suggesting that, if they felt that I was worthy of the award, then he described how they should go about registering my nomination. It turned out that I received more nominations that any previous candidate for the award.

As a result of this, the Chef Executive of the GCMA and one of the sponsors of the scheme visited the club to meet with various officers and I was invited to attend. However, after a short while, I asked to be excused from the meeting as I was finding it uncomfortable in hearing all the things they had to say about me.

Following that visit, I made the shortlist as one of the six candidates for the award and was invited for some golf at Burnham & Berrow Golf Club and then a final interview with a panel of eight assessors for the award.

From speaking to the other candidates, they had all been nominated for one particular piece of management whereas, I couldn't pin my nomination on anything in particular but hoped that my all round impact on the club would suffice.

Not that I expected to win, I was more than pleased that I had achieved my second objective in my golf club career.

With the Annual General Meeting over, the announcement of the award was made. There were only two prizes up for grabs, the runner up and the winner which obviously meant that four candidates would leave with only the honour of having been nominated.

The first name read out, as the runner up – was ME!

Whilst a little disappointed that I'd not won, I realised it was a great achievement, especially as I had only been in the position for a short while. Notwithstanding that, I was soon brought down to earth on my return home when my eldest son suggested that my position in the award was that of First Loser!

Monday 9th May 2011

The usual procedure for dealing with the death of a current member is to fly the flag at half mast (* see note below), display notices in the clubhouse and on the website, notify the other current members and send a card of condolence to the family of the deceased. Notices would be updated when details of the funeral arrangements became available. When notified of the death of a past member of the club, current members would be notified and asked if they wished to be informed of the funeral arrangements when available. Once the funeral had taken place, all of the above would be removed.

The first of only two occasions when the flag was flown at half mast for a non-member was when Severiano Ballesteros of Spain passed away.

He had actually passed away in the early hours of Saturday morning and news had filtered through over the weekend. This followed being diagnosed with a malignant brain tumour two and a half years previously. During that time, he had undergone four operations and while, at times, there was hope that he would survive, he suffered a severe deterioration the day before his untimely passing. He was aged just 54.

As well as a personal hero, Seve is widely acknowledged to have been the foundation upon which European golf was re-built in the late seventies/early eighties. Not only through his flair and creativity on the golf course but also through his record of individual success and of course, his contribution to the success of the European team in the Ryder Cup.

RIP Seve.

Note – I believe that there is a misinterpretation of the term half mast. Firstly, my understanding is that the term should be haf mast and that the flag, rather than being lowered to halfway down the flagpole, should be lowered to one width of a flag down the pole to accommodate the 'invisible flag of death'.

Tuesday 24th July 2011

So here's one of those occasions where I have to relay an experience that has some bearing with the playing of the game of golf.

I've played today with my two sons at the club where I work. In the car on the way home, they were very complementary about the condition of the golf course and the way it was playing. Obviously, I thanked them for their comments, but I remarked on how none of us had holed any putts beyond a three foot distance.

My eldest son replied saying that was because the holes on the course were much smaller than those where they usually play. My youngest son concurred with that view.

This reminded me of a conversation we had previously had at a meeting with the Greens Committee when it was relayed to us that a member had made the same comments – I have to say that this had had us all in stitches because we couldn't see how it was possible as the tool used to cut holes is a standard size to ensure that the Rules of Golf are adhered to.

Anyway, to cut a long story short, it transpired that the member of staff responsible for that job and using too much brute force when the hole had been cut that the effect was to reduce the size of the hole!!!

We kept that one quiet and changed the procedure for changing holes!!

Thursday 11ᵗʰ August 2011

On my journey home from the Golf Club Manager of the Year announcement in April, I had decided to introduce a fourth objective into my golf club management career – play for England Golf Club Managers in an international match.

When I returned to the office, I called the Chief Executive to tell him and, to cut a long story short, I was selected to play against Scotland at Spey Valley Golf Club in Aviemore – and the match is today!

I travelled to Scotland a day early in order to have a night in St Andrews but before arriving there, I played at the former Open Championship venue just outside Edinburgh – Musselburgh Links.

I camped overnight in St Andrews before heading north on the A9 to Aviemore the following morning. On arrival, I joined up with the rest of the players from both teams and a practice round was held in the afternoon before dinner that evening.

The following day, two rounds of golf were to be played (morning and afternoon) and I'm pleased to report that my partner and I won both of our matches. The victories came easier than they should have done as one of our opponents was suffering from the 'yips', a state of extreme nervousness when putting.

Sadly, England lost the match but it was great to be involved.

Thursday 25th August 2011

The Professional has been a wonderful servant to this golf club as the celebration for his silver anniversary of his tenure attests last year.

His father has passed away recently and so the Captain and I agree that we will attend today's funeral to represent the club and show our support for the Professional.

The Captain of the day was a lovely man and I got on very well with him. I even played a couple of games of golf with him as he established a relationship with his counterpart at

Burton-on-Trent Golf Club. However, as lovely as he was, he wasn't the best when it came to playing golf!

The funeral service was beautiful and one of those where there were no hymns sung.

As we left the chapel, I turned to the Captain and told him that he'd had a lucky break there. When he asked why, I told him that my singing was worse than his golf!

Wednesday 7th September 2011

There are two main exhibitions in the turf management industry – the British Turf Management Exhibition (BTME) which is held in Harrogate in the early part of the year and then Saltex which is held in Windsor during the Autumn.

Today, I'm visiting the Saltex Exhibition. I visited BTME on a number of occasions so thought I would visit here to compare the two.

Now I can't really explain why I went to the first seminar as it was nothing to do with turf management or golf! Maybe it was just the attraction of seeing Olympic athletes Steve Backley and Roger Black?

Nor can I explain why they were there but nevertheless, I went along and with only eleven others in that seminar, it was like having a one to one session with them.

There lecture surrounded motivation and how it never give up to realise your dreams, goals and ambitions. I made as many notes as I could to relay to my sons for them to take heed of as they develop their golf game. In fact, I'd looked at the following days schedule and if they had been on again, I would have kept the boys off school and taken them to see it!

It was a fabulous experience.

There was an additional benefit to attending this seminar. My wife has always had a little crush on Steve Backley and so I obtained his autograph and he added 'Happy Anniversary' as it is our wedding anniversary next week. That sorted my present out for another year!

Tuesday 11th October 2011

We now have a new problem with the Sewerage Treatment Plant that was installed as a replacement to the Reed Bed.

It is located at the bottom of the hill of the 18th hole and yesterday, it rained and it rained and it rained!!

The result was that the water coming off the hill all found its way towards the Sewerage Treatment Plant causing the new problem – the water level in the plant overall has reached flood level and all the media that is in the secondary treatment chamber and breach the top and spilled over into the other two chambers!!

This has meant that today, I've brought to work my waterproofs and my daughter's fishing net so I can lay down, fish the media out of the first and final chambers and restore it to the secondary chamber where it rightfully belongs!!

My greatest concern is that my glasses don't fall off and land in one of the three tanks - but I needn't have worried!

Friday 9th December 2011

It's Christmas Open day again today but it's touch and go!

The weather leading up to today has been fine but yesterday, it was dreadful and the event hangs in the balance.

I'm at the club at 6.00am and I'm continually seeing what the weather is doing and checking the weather forecasts. By

7.00am, I'm joined by the Caterer and the Head Greenkeeper, and amongst our conversations as to whether we should go ahead or not, we continue to check the weather outside and the forecast for the rest of the day. By 7.30am, we're starting to get calls from competitors asking if the open is going ahead.

At 7.45am, I realise that someone has to make a decision. I also realise that that someone is going to be me!

I decide that we're going ahead on the basis that the forecast for the day says there's going to be an improvement in the weather and the Caterer has food ready to feed one hundred and twenty people.

Having made the decision, the website is updated so anyone checking that knows the decision, the course information line on the telephone system is also changed to reflect the decision and all those that have called are phoned to tell them that the event is on.

In the end, the decision to go ahead was the right one and we got away with it! Phew!

Sunday 1st January 2012

It's Captain's Drive in day again today and all goes to schedule.

The Captain announces that his charity for the year will be the Harley Staples Cancer Trust. This is a charity in memory of Harley Staples who died in 2009, aged just eight. He died from a rare leukaemia B Cell Acute Lymphoblastic Leukaemia Burkitt type.

While Harley was poorly, people wanted to help and fundraising began in case Harley needed to travel elsewhere for treatment and also so that he could have special treats. As it happened there was no more treatment left that Harley could have had anywhere in the world so because they had accumulated quite a sum of money, it was decided to register the charity in August 2010.

The family was known to member of the golf club and he, in turn, had brought it to the attention of the Captain who had no hesitation in selecting it as his charity for the year.

The main objective was to raise sufficient funds to enable the charity to purchase a holiday home which would welcome children and young adults with cancer, along with their families, to enjoy quality time together in a homely environment.

As well as the usual fundraising activities and events, a special golf event was planned for the summer…..

Monday 20th February 2012

When the Chairman arrived this morning for his usual Monday morning meeting, he opened with asking if the rubbish that had been dumped on the road outside, and therefore at the side of the golf course, could be removed and disposed of. It must have been recent as it wasn't there when I arrived for work.

Before our meeting began, I called the Head Greenkeeper and asked if he could send a couple of the lads down there in a truck to collect it up and he agreed.

Once the meeting had been completed, I had to speak to the Head Greenkeeper and therefore headed up to the sheds. When there, he confirmed that it had been collected although at that time, the rubbish was still in the back of the truck.

He then said, "You know what it is don't you?" I had a closer look but had no idea what it was. I must have led a sheltered life as he informed me that it was a cannabis factory!

On receipt of this information, I called the police to inform them what had happened and what I had and I was asked to take it to the police station.

Now I have to say that I never gave it any thought whatsoever as I piled this stuff into my car. It was only when I was on my way to the police station that it dawned on me what I was doing! I do remember calling my wife to tell her. I'd opened the conversation by informing her that I wasn't hands free in using my mobile telephone but that was the least of my problems!

I arrived at the police station, without being stopped (!) and headed straight to the reception desk to explain what had happened and what I had in my car.

The desk clerk was outraged that I had been asked to transport it to them and I believe that serious questions were being asked at their end.

I emptied the cannabis factory from my car, left it in their reception as instructed and never heard another word about it!

Whilst not recommending it, it was the best air freshener my car had had in years!

Saturday 28th April 2012

Now I have to confess at the outset that this news item doesn't really have anything to do with my role as a Golf Club Manager other than playing golf at the course that I work.

Some months previously, I had been asked if my sons would represent the club in a match but I declined on the basis that they weren't members! I didn't think it would look good on me or the club or them if that fact subsequently came out. As a result, I asked the Management Committee for courtesy memberships for them both so that if they were asked again in the future, they could do so. My request was unanimously agreed, albeit on the basis that they could win any competition they entered at my insistence. I did not want them to take any of the spoils that a member that had paid their dues was entitled to.

During the winter of 2011/12, both sons had been coached within an inch of their lives through the County and also with England and that included Warm Winter Training in Portugal.

By the end of April, they were desperate to get a scorecard in their hand and therefore I invited them to play in the monthly strokeplay competition with me.

Not only did they both come in under par and beat the field by miles, they both scored twenty three strokes lower than I did!

It did nothing to enhance my reputation on the golf course and my claims of teaching them all I know fell on stony ground!

Wednesday 16th May 2012

Another catering complaint puts a black cloud over the day – there's too much mayonnaise in the tuna mayo!

Really? I can't grasp the concept of too much mayonnaise!

Friday 22nd June 2012

Following the announcement that the Harley Staples Cancer Trust was to be the Captain's selected charity for the year at the Drive In on New Year's Day, a special fundraising golf event was organised for today.

Sixteen members, including the Captain – and myself – set out at 4.30am to play eighteen holes of golf in one day. However, although many people have undertaken similar projects but ours had a difference – we would play on four different courses!

We started out on the first course and played nine holes, got in our cars and went to the second course to play eighteen holes and after that, went to course number three to play a further eighteen. Then, due to other commitments on the other courses, we went to the fourth course to play nine, return to the first course to play the second nine and then returned to the fourth course, our home club, to play the final nine holes. The day ended shortly after 9.00pm.

To say that the sixteen of us were shattered was the understatement of the day but a good time had been had by all and we have provided a welcome boost to the Captain's fundraising efforts for the Harley Staples Cancer Trust.

Thursday 19th July 2012

I shouldn't have been at work today!

I should have been in the middle of a two week break from work – my first since 2003.

This week, I was scheduled to be in Cornwall all week to support my youngest son as he competed in the McGregor

Trophy (England Golf's Under 16 Strokeplay Championship). Then next week, I'm in Kent to support my eldest son as he competes in the Carris Trophy (England Golf's Under 18 Strokeplay Championship).

The problem was that my youngest son didn't score well enough in the first two days of his competition and therefore didn't qualify for the final two rounds so we returned home early.

Rather than remain off work, I had decided to come in today and tomorrow to make sure that there wasn't anything that needed to be attended to urgently, particularly as I'm off again next week. I can then take those two days as some point where all the family can be together.

I had text the Chairman to let him know that I would be in and shortly after lunch, he came in for a meeting.

At some point, that meeting got a little heated as he questioned a working practice that was in place. He went on to add that, as a former Management Consultant, he had often considered coming in to the office for a day to do a 'time and motion' study on me.

At that point, I asked for a brief adjournment. I went to the office, collected my diary and then returned to him. I asked him when he was coming as, like many Chairman, he hadn't got a clue what my job entailed.

He declined to arrange a date, never did come in to do his study and never mentioned it again.

Wednesday 29th August 2012

Now this is a real unusual occurrence!

There's been a lot of rain of late and the fairway on the fourth hole has become saturated and there is no water draining away. We found that the land drains had collapsed and therefore needed renewal.

The team has been working on putting new drains in for a week and I going to have a walk down there to assess the progress they are making.

As it is raining, I'd been the changing room to don my waterproof gear and golf shoes and set off in the company of one of the Management Committee.

When we're about half way, we can't help but notice that a helicopter is circling the golf course but give it no further thought.

After seeing the work, which by the way, looked a complete and utter mess, I walked back to the clubhouse, went to the changing room to return to my work gear and then went to the office.

On arrival, my Assistant told me that the police had called and as I wasn't available, they were sending two officers round to see me and it wasn't long before they duly arrived.

The story was that just before the school behind the 18th tee opened for the day, three teachers had gone to the bottom of their garden for a last cigarette. Whilst one of them was sitting on one of the garden seats, a 'bullet' had hit one of the legs causing the fear that a sniper was on the loose – hence the use of the police helicopter.

My first reaction was that 'they say smoking will kill you' which, fortunately, the officers saw as being funny.

The only plausible explanation we came up with was that the club's shooter (most clubs have them to keep vermin under control) had been in that area at that time of day. He had taken a shot and it had ricocheted off a stone or rock and sent his missile in the general direction of the smoking teachers.

Our shooter was naturally very upset at this allegation and even offered to take his rifle into the police for a ballistics check (do they really do that or is that something I've dreamt up after watching American TV?!).

There was nothing ever proved one way or the other and the matter was dropped (and it never did reoccur!).

In fact, the only outcome of this issue was for me to take flowers to the three teachers involved, together with a bunch for the Head Mistress.

Tuesday 25th September 2012

We've all heard reports and forecasts about future weather conditions and the effects of global warming and this is particularly felt in golfing circles where water is needed during the summer months to maintain and develop putting greens.

As a result of this, we've been investigating options available to us and more specifically about installing a borehole. We see the benefits as being a continuous supply of water whilst keeping the costs under control by avoiding the need to use supplies from the mains.

We have therefore held an initial meeting with a supplier and installer of boreholes today so that we can assess its cost and usefulness to us in the future.

Thursday 27th September 2012

As a follow on from the previously reported Captain's fundraising for the Harley Staples Cancer Trust (HSCT), Persimmon Homes, to celebrate their 40th anniversary in house building, had offered to give away a house worth £250000 to a charity. The charity was one of over 3,000 nominations for the prize, and made it through to the 24 finalists. At that point, there was a public vote and all the public had to do was go online and register their free vote for one of the finalists.

Having become aware of this, I voted everyday until the closing date and regularly reminded members to also vote.

Today, the winner was announced and out of the 130000 votes cast, the Harley Staples Cancer Trust emerged as the winners. The house, which was located in Andover, Hampshire, was to be sold in order to raise further funds towards achieving the target of opening the holiday home which would welcome children and young adults with cancer, along with their families, to enjoy quality time together in a homely environment.

Thursday 1st November 2012

Like a lot of golf clubs during the winter months, we struggle to get people into the clubhouse to continue to support the food and beverage functions, particularly when the weather it at its worst and specifically when the golf course is closed.

In order to try and provide some reason to visit, I've introduced putting competitions in the clubhouse, bingo and numerous other initiatives.

Today, saw the delivery of two table tennis tables to add further encouragement to come to the club. I'd had a number of requests for such equipment and managed to convince the Management Committee to provide funds to allow the purchase and they obviously agreed.

As we were at Lingdale playing ping pong, this activity was known as 'Ling Pong'!

Friday 7th December 2012

It's Christmas Open day and after last year's 'will we won't we' situation, the weather leading up to the event is fine and everything goes ahead as scheduled.

Sunday 23rd December 2012

I've had the pleasure of sleeping in the clubhouse overnight!

We've had a problem with the heating system and have, as yet, been unable to resolve it. As it's winter, there aren't as many people visiting the clubhouse and so with the heating going down, it's cooling down and we have a big function on today.

In order to provide a quick fix to the situation, I'd been and purchased four oil filled radiators so they could be left on overnight and keep the room reasonably warm. The trouble was, I didn't want to leave them unsupervised so decided to stay. I know there are lots of electrical appliances we leave on all the time, but felt that these were different in that their intended use was to generate heat.

The night went relatively smoothly, apart from the time I recalled rumours of ghosts and being haunted!!

Still rather being at home with the family, I at least had the television remote control all to myself for the evening!

Tuesday 1st January 2013

As is tradition, the newly installed Captain announces that his nominated charity for the year will be another fundraising year for the Harley Staples Cancer Trust.

Wednesday 20th February 2013

It was nearing 7.00 a.m. when I was within half a mile from the entrance to the golf club.

The main road outside the club is not lit and as we're almost in the middle of nowhere, it's very dark. On either side of the entrance to the club, there are a series of reflective posts on the grass verge to indicate where the driveway is.

As I approach, there is a gathering of people, together with a breakdown truck!

One of the senior members that plays early doors on a Wednesday morning had mistaken the reflective posts and rather than drive in between them, had turned before the first set and then straight into the ditch!

The Greenkeepers were out in force to help him as best they could before my arrival and thankfully, he was alright. Although the same couldn't be said about his car!

Thursday 14th March 2013

I have an appointment this morning with a representative of the printing company we use to have our club diary printed. We want to explore other printing opportunities to further promote the club and our brand.

The gentleman is a lovely guy and we've always got on very well. In addition, I have much respect for him as during a previous meeting, I found out that he used to be a professional footballer back in the day with Blackpool.

We meet in the office and at the outset, I offer him the chance of having a cuppa – a very unusual occurrence for me. I only ever offer when I've asked to see someone (and not always then) and never offer when someone has asked to see me!

As he accepts my offer, I ask my Assistant that is on that day to make coffee for two and he leaves to go to the kitchen.

Our meeting proceeds, but after some while, I've realised that my Assistant is not back with the coffee and if I'm not careful, the meeting will be over before the coffee arrives.

I call the kitchen to find out where it is but there is no answer so I excuse myself from the meeting to find out what has happened but can't find my Assistant anywhere.

I returned to the office, apologise for leaving the meeting and for that fact that the coffee has not arrived and continue with the meeting.

After about another fifteen minutes, the Assistant returned to the office with coffee for two as requested. I ask why it has taken so long and he explains that he needed to go to the toilet and when he got there, he realised that he needed a 'Number 2'!

The representative and I just looked at each other in amazement at what we'd just been told.

After he had gone, I had to explain that his description of the delay fell under the category of 'too much information'!

Wednesday 15th May 2013

Today, I find myself at Everards Brewery though there won't be any tasting or sampling going on!

Most golf clubs have been traditionally licensed to sell alcoholic drinks by applying for a Club Premises Certificate and to be fair, that's worked fine for many years. However, in the push to generate additional revenue from their clubhouses and bars, which are largely underutilised, golf clubs are wanting to open their doors to more non members and non member events, both of which really call for a more open Premises Licence.

In order for my club to obtain their Premises Licence, they have to appoint a Designated Premises Supervisor who has obtained a Personal Licence to sell alcohol – and that's why I'm at the brewery today.

The day is scheduled to be in part a training course and then there's an examination at the end that will determine a pass or fail and therefore the issue of a Personal Licence.

A good day was had by all and a pass followed for me at least.

Thursday 20th June 2013

It's getting close to 10.00pm when my mobile phone starts ringing. It's one of the bar staff at the golf club who is concerned that a couple in a mobile home have been given permission by a member of the Management Committee to park up for the night. The story was given was that they were a German couple – father and daughter. She had been playing golf in Scotland but were on the way home to Germany. They had booked to play golf at our club the following morning and as a result, had made the request to stay over.

The bar staff had called me as she was concerned about having visitors around when locking up at the close of business. I asked her to leave it with me.

On ending the call, I checked our online timesheet for the following day and as there were no visitors booked in, I immediately also had concerns, contacted the club to say I was on my way and then got in my car for the forty minute journey.

On arrival, I knocked on the door of the mobile home and the father answered. I introduced myself and then told him that there had been a breakdown in communications at the club and that I had to ask him to move on. Naturally, I apologised for the inconvenience.

To be fair, he did take it on the chin and began arrangements to move which he did, no doubt on the basis that his claim that he had a time booked for golf the following morning wasn't entirely true!

I waited around the club for a while to ensure he hadn't just moved off to return shortly after but he didn't.

Friday 21st June 2013

As a result of last night's excitement, I field two telephone calls – one from the member of the Management Committee that had given permission for them to stay and the other from the Chairman who had been alerted of the situation. Both wanted to ensure that everything was alright at the club.

I informed them that everything was ok as a result of my late night intervention and the fact that we are a golf club and not a caravanning and camping park.

Saturday 22nd June 2013

It's Captain's Day here today but there's been a difference!

Yesterday, the Vice Captain had set up a large gazebo on the Practice Ground, filled it with the drinks and food required for today's event, but to make sure the contents didn't get stolen overnight, five of us camped inside to guard them.

Our evening consisted of a barbeque and an excess of alcohol, which was followed by five holes of golf – in the dark! The Captain had purchased some florescent golf balls that could be seen in the dark and we had great fun, particularly as the Vice Captain, worse for wear through drink at this stage, managed to lose one of the balls!

On hearing of our midnight golf antics, a Past Captain asked me who was looking after the contents of the gazebo while we were out playing? Good question!!

The other memorable aspect of the night was the sheer terror experienced by the youngest of the group. He'd never camped before and was scared stiff at the prospect of being alone (even with us) in a remote field in the middle of nowhere. It didn't help that we did all we could to ensure that his terror was well placed!

Saturday 17th August 2013

I've got some friends together, including my mother, to attend a social evening at the golf club – a jazz band, one of which is a member of the club. A meal is included.

We pile into three cars to make the twenty-mile journey to the golf club and I swear that when we arrived, it was the last time I saw them until it was time to go home. It confirmed my suspicions that no one saw you as being off duty and therefore, I was up and down like a yo-yo after being asked to do various tasks during the evening, including acting as compeer for the show.

On Monday morning, when I generally meet the Chairman, I'm going to tell him that I'm not attending anymore – I could have gone to somewhere much nearer home and had a full night with them, rather than hardly seeing them. It's not that I don't want to support the club and I'll happily go along and work if that's required, but if I'm going for a social, then I'm going for a social.

Sunday 15th September 2013

This afternoon, there's a social event on at the club – a Golfer / Non-Golfer competition followed by a meal.

I've invited my daughter to join me and we're playing with the Captain and his wife.

The concept of the competition is that the golfer will get the ball to the green and then the non-golfer will finish the hole by putting out.

Clearly, I'm in the role of the golfer (though my sons would argue with that!) and my daughter takes the role of the non-golfer.

Being super competitive, I've worked out a strategy for victory!! When playing the hole, I'll deliberately just miss the green so that I can chip/pitch up closer to the hole to give my daughter shorter putts.

The theory was spot on – the practical less so. I'm not that good a golfer! Needless to say, we didn't win but we did have a thoroughly enjoyable afternoon.

Friday 6th December 2013

Today, it's the Christmas Open again and everything goes ahead according to schedule and there were no problems with the weather.

In fact, we add an additional feature this year where I dressed up as Santa Claus to hand out the prizes to the winners of the event.

At one point in the presentation, the Captain hands me the microphone and I say "that although it's Christmas, I have today made one New Year's Resolution – and that's to check my job description to see if dressing up as Santa Claus is included!"

The Chairman of the Management Committee, who was in the audience, subsequently confirmed to me that it was!

Wednesday 1st January 2014

As is tradition, the newly installed Captain announces that his nominated charity for the year will be one last push for the Harley Staples Cancer Trust.

Wednesday 28th May 2014

It's the inaugural match where the club is playing a team from Battleback, a programme that utilises golf to enhance the recovery of wounded, injured and sick service personnel to rehabilitate.

It is a scheme very dear to my heart as the son of a good friend lost the bottom half of his leg as a result of an incendiary device whilst on patrol in Afghanistan.

The result of the match was immaterial as we saw how these servicemen had overcome their injuries to go on and lead full and meaningful lives.

Friday 30th May 2014

My last day at Lingdale Golf Club.

When starting out in golf club management, I'd set out with three objectives;-

i) Get a job
ii) Be nominated for Golf Club Manager of the Year within five years and
iii) Secure an appointment at a golf club that hosts The Open.

You will have become aware from earlier references in this book that I had achieved the first two objectives but to achieve the third, I believed that I would have to move to a club further up the golf club pyramid.

That's not meant to be any disrespect to Lingdale but I felt that they didn't host enough high profile events to bring me to the powers that be.

As a result, in addition to a number of other jobs, I had applied for the position of Business Manager at the West Lancashire Golf Club (known as West Lancs), just north of

Liverpool and I was successful with that application, and I duly accepted.

As already stated, today was my last day at Lingdale. I'd largely tied up all the loose ends that needed to be tied up and had removed all of my personal possessions.

The main focus of today was a leaving presentation where the Captain said a few kind words about me and my time there and I reciprocated with a presentation of my own, not only reflecting on my time at Lingdale but also looking forward to the new position at West Lancs.

Everything went very well, a good few members turned out to bid me farewell and I rode off into the sunset for a new dawn in my golf management career.

Chapter 2

West Lancashire Golf Club
Blundellsands, Lancashire

Business Manager

2nd June 2014 – 24th October 2014

West Lancashire Golf Club

The club prides itself in being one of the oldest clubs in England, having been formed in 1873. It was formed to provide an alternative golfing experience for the members of Royal Liverpool Golf Club (Hoylake) just a few miles away.

The course is a traditional links course i.e. where it has been developed in the strip between the sea and the land and, like many golf clubs, saw its development as a result of its close proximity to the railway that follows the coastline.

Its main claim to fame in the early days was that, in 1885, it was one of the original subscribers to the cost of the Amateur Championship Trophy and the first winner of the trophy was a member of the club.

In 1889, Harold Hilton joined the club as a member and he would go on to win the Open Championship in 1892 and 1897. He also won the British Amateur on four occasions and also he was crowned US Amateur Champion in 1911. In 1901, Harold had become the first paid Secretary of the club.

In the intervening years, the club has hosted most of the leading amateur golf championships in addition to being the venue for Regional Qualifying and Final Qualifying competitions for the Open Championship.

Monday 2nd June 2014.

The first day at my new club in the North West.

The first thing that struck me was how big this job was going to be!! It was like going back in time. Some of the tasks being completed were so long and laborious (without the use of technology) that it was clear that it was going to take much longer to get it in 'ship shape and Bristol fashion'.

After that first day's work had been completed, I visited Anfield, the home of Liverpool Football Club, to take the flowers I had bought at lunchtime to the Hillsborough Memorial and Eternal Flame. It was erected in memory of the ninety six supporters that lost their lives At the F.A. Cup semi final in 1989. As a supporter of Nottingham Forest, Liverpool's opponents that day, I was at Hillsborough and the date of 15th April is now forever etched in my mind.

Sunday 13th July 2014

In what has very definitely one of my highlights in golf club management was the hosting of the Royal & Ancient's (R&A)

Junior Open. This competition is held every two years and at a course near to where the Open Championship is being held – this year, it is at Royal Liverpool.

The Junior Open is for golfers under the age of sixteen and each country that is affiliated to the R&A is asked to send one boy and one girl to compete in the event. When it was held at the club that I was working at, one hundred and twenty five competitors represented seventy five countries. They were accommodated at Edge Hill University and transported to the club for each day of play.

Today was the Opening Ceremony for the event, which comprised of each of the competitors being introduced to a large crowd, with speeches from a representative from the R&A and the Captain of the club. They then had the opportunity to hold the Claret Jug, the trophy that would be awarded to the winner of The Open the following weekend.

Later that evening, and once the children had been returned to their accommodation, the delegates from the countries being represented had been invited to a Gala Dinner at the club where a sumptuous four course dinner was served. I had the pleasure of sitting with the delegates from Panama, Latvia, Namibia and Mauritius and golf in some of those countries is not as we know it!

At the conclusion of the dinner, I was approached by a representative of the R&A who carrying a wooden box. I was asked if I could look after it until the following day when it would be collected the following day and transported to Royal Liverpool for the Open Championship – it was the Claret Jug!!

I was aware that it is not the original, as that is kept on permanent display in St Andrews, but nevertheless, it was quite a responsibility to be the custodian even if for just one night and I was mightily relieved to pass it on the following morning.

Couldn't resist the opportunity of a photograph with the Claret Jug before I put it away for safekeeping overnight. The next time I'd see it was when it was being handed to Rory McIlroy on winning The Open at Royal Liverpool.

Wednesday 16th July 2014

The final round of the Junior Open has been completed with a very worthy winner. We received very complimentary comments on the condition of the golf course and for the hospitality arrangements we had in place for the event.

The closing ceremony followed and the Captain and I received a plaque from the R&A on behalf of the club to commemorate the hosting of the tournament.

Thursday 17th July 2014

It's really starting to come home to me of the benefits of being at a more prestigious club as today, we have four VIP guests on the golf course – the four main people at the United States Professional Golf Association, including their President.

They are in the UK to take in the Open Championship as we're just down the road, they come to play.

Whilst we're not making a charge for their golf, they have paid for caddies for their round and arrangements have been made for lunch when they have finished.

We hadn't been asked to make provision for them hitting a few balls before they played though and as they arrived before the Professional's Shop opened, I found myself collecting as many balls as I could from the practice areas so they could warm up prior to golf!

Notwithstanding that, it was a huge privilege to have been host to them on that day and of course, I did not miss the photo opportunity their visit presented!

Sunday 20th July 2014

As one of the benefits of being involved with the hosting of the Junior Open, I received complimentary tickets to attend the Open Championship at Royal Liverpool for the Saturday and Sunday – a welcome rest after the week's exertions in managing that event.

It goes without saying that as I watched on from the grandstand around the 18th green, the trophy was handed to Northern Ireland's Rory McIlroy the following Sunday as the winner, having withstood the challenges of Spain's Sergio Garcia and Ricky Fowler from the USA.

Even better though was the fact that through connections at the golf club, I had managed to obtain work for both of my sons at the Open in driving the Outside Broadcast cameramen around the course to film the action for the BBC. They both were able to be around the eighteenth green when the prize presentation was held and Rory received the Claret Jug.

Thursday 31st July 2014

The club I'm at place strong emphasis on their heritage and last night, one of the Past Captain's gave a talk on the club's association with the two World Wars.

I had helped him set up the various Powerpoint slides and had even borrowed the projector from my previous club as the one where I am now was about as good as a chocolate fireguard.
The meeting overran by some considerable distance and by the time I got away after packing everything away, it was getting very late.

Before turning in, I had two further jobs to do. The first was to ring home, as I did every evening, just to share information from the day. The second was to get something to eat as I'd not had anything since lunchtime.

With both jobs done, I headed back to my accommodation for the evening and bed but there was a problem – I was locked out!!

I tried calling the mobile number I had but without success and I didn't have a landline number. I was also conscious that it was very late and didn't want to make any noise for fear of upsetting the neighbours.

There was only one thing left to do – drive back to the club car park and sleep in the car! (I didn't want to go into the clubhouse as that would have meant that the alarm wouldn't be set for the night and I was certain that Sod's Law would apply and that there would be an incident.

Now sleep in the car was very much an overstatement as I found that, at that time, I owned the most uncomfortable car for sleeping in!

Little sleep came my way and I was delighted when daylight arrived and I could go into the clubhouse and have a shower and change.

Don't think that today will go on for too long!

Tuesday 12th August 2014

Before I recall today's meeting with the Chairman, I need to tell you about one of the staff working here – Mr Versatility.

Whilst primarily employed as a cleaner and janitor (for want of a better word), Mr Versatility could turn his hand to anything including donning a shirt and tie and working behind the bar or waiting on. He one of those workers that is invaluable to any team in being flexible enough to help out where help is needed.

As it's Tuesday, it's the day for the weekly meeting with the Chairman and his sidekick. I was never quite sure why his sidekick was his sidekick because he really didn't like him. In fact, I'm not sure whether anybody did! Perhaps it came under the banner of keeping your enemies close?

The meeting usually consisting of going through the endless reports and returns we had to produce on a Monday in readiness for this meeting – talk about 'paralysis by analysis'!

Once that part of the meeting had ended, the Chairman went on to tell me that he was in the bar the previous week when his playing partner noted that Mr versatility was serving behind the bar and mentioned to the Chairman that he thought he was employed as a cleaner/janitor.

The Chairman expressed disappointment that he didn't have an answer for his playing partner.

I did know which day he was talking about. On the day in question, the bar staff on the rota for that morning had rang in sick and their replacement couldn't get in until a couple of hours after the scheduled bar opening time. As a result, I had asked Mr Versatility to man the bar until the replacement arrived.

I retorted that he did have an answer.

The Chairman replied that he hadn't.

I again stated that he did.

The Chairman then asked what his answer was.

I told him that the answer was that he employed a Manager to deploy staff to ensure the best effectiveness of the business and that if, at that time, the Manager deemed that Mr Versatility was best being used as a bar person (and therefore generating income) rather than a cleaner/janitor (and therefore not generating income), then that's why he was behind the bar.

The Chairman then ended the meeting and then left without saying another word!

Thursday 18th September 2014

I mentioned earlier that the first time I had lowered the flag for a non-member was following the death of Severiano Ballesteros in 2011. I also mentioned that this had only occurred on two occasions – today was the second.

Our Head Greenkeeper had passed away following a long battle with cancer.

I enjoyed an excellent relationship with him whilst he was at work but he had spent most of his final days in hospital receiving treatment. On my return to the area on a Sunday evening after a weekend at home, I used to call in and see him in hospital.

Friday 26th September 2014

The club has a great tradition with all of the forces and has regularly played hosts to their National Championships and Inter Forces matches. Notwithstanding that, they're probably closest to the Royal Navy and understandably seeing as the docks in Liverpool are only four miles south of here.

Yesterday, we hosted a match between the club and the Royal Navy and that had been organised as a result of the latter donating a bust of Johnnie Walker to the former.

Now this Johnnie Walker is not to be confused with the famous Scotch whisky that was founded in Kilmarnock, East Ayrshire by Scottish grocer, John Walker. 'Our' Johnnie Walker was born Frederic John Walker and was a Royal Navy officer most noted for his exploits during World War 11. He was the most successful anti-submarine warfare commander during the Battle of the Atlantic but did eventually become known as 'Johnnie' after the brand of whisky.

He was born in 1896 in Plymouth and joined the Royal Navy as a cadet in 1909. He became an expert in anti-submarine warfare in the period leading up to World War 11. By the time that arrived, it appeared that his naval career was at an end, having been passed over for promotion on a number of occasions. However, he was mentioned in despatches for his role in Operation Dynamo, the evacuation of 330,000 English and French troops from Dunkirk and as a result, he was given his own command and therefore, the opportunity to test his innovative methods against the threat of U-boats. Due to his success, he was given commands of various ships that eventually saw him settle in the Liverpool area.

He died in 1944 following a cerebral thrombosis in the Naval Hospital just outside Liverpool.

The match, which included the Commodore playing for the Royal Navy, was won by the club and the Captain was duly presented with the bust of Johnnie Walker.

A new tradition has been created and it is envisaged that this match will now be an annual event.

Monday 6th October 2014

Notwithstanding the deaths and funerals during my time as a golf club manager, this is probably the saddest day of my career to date.

Over the weekend when I've been back home, I've been speaking to my family about resigning my position and having had those discussions, I've decided to quit.

Such is the Chairman's ferocity to transform the club, I left fearful that I'll be pushed and so I've decided to jump ship before it gets to that.

As well as saddened, I'm really really disappointed as I remain convinced that I'm the man to turn the club around. With a little more time and with a little more freedom, I would have got the done but he is seeking revolution and not evolution and I have no faith that I'm going to be given that time.

As I've come to that decision, I arrive in the office this morning and email him my decision but give three week's notice rather than the contractual one. Despite the sadness and the disappointment, I want to tie up loose ends and ensure that those left behind have sufficient knowledge of where I am with certain aspects of the work.

Wednesday 8th October 2014

When I first arrived at the club, they were in the process of installing a new theft detection system which involved a steam machine clouding the room where trophies are kept on display.

Basically, once the alarm has been triggered, the system is activated, and the room is filled with smoke in seconds so that any would be thieves would be unable to see.

We lived with a hole in the roof for weeks before finally seeing it in action for the first time today.

Friday 17th October 2014

I receive a call from the Chairman saying that he will call and see me during the morning and obviously that was not a problem (although he didn't make it until lunchtime – time management was never one of his strong points!).

The view amongst the other staff was that he was coming to see me to try and talk me out of my decision and get me to stay on. However, I was less than convinced.

When he arrived, he handed me a letter, which I opened while he was there and basically, he was saying he wanted me to go today!!

I explained to him that there were still things I needed to sort out before leaving the following week, had appointments booked in my diary and, most importantly, I couldn't return to my accommodation to collect my things as he had left it too late to come and see me!

As a result, I'll be in work next week.

Wednesday 22nd October 2014

Whilst I've been at West Lancs, I've been working with a Past Captain to detail the history of the golf club on the website with the help of my daughter.

One of the photos I've taken to add to that history is of a display cabinet in the Ladies Changing Room that contains clothing worn by ladies during that era of golf.

I've included this photograph as, in the top left just above the hat, you can see my reflection in the display cabinet glass!! My Alfred Hitchcock moment!!

Friday 24th October 2014

Since the visit of the movers and shakers from the United States Professional Golf Association (USPGA) in July, I've been kicking myself that I didn't try to exert some influence in arranging a round of golf for my sons and myself at Augusta National, Georgia where the U.S. Masters is played every year.

It's probably the one course that the vast majority of amateur golfers want to play, probably because of a combination of its exclusivity and the fact that it is the one course we see every year as it is the only venue that acts as a permanent home to one of the four major competitions – US Masters, US Open, The Open and the US PGA Championship.

Anyway, today, the breaking news is that the President of the USPGA has been axed after 'insensitive, gender-based' comments aimed at a professional golfer!

Seems that that opportunity has now gone anyway!

Friday 24th October 2014

So it's my last day here.

My in-tray and pending trays are all cleared and my accommodation has been emptied. Basically, I'm going to use the morning to say goodbye to the staff and then I'm off at lunchtime. At least, I'll miss the worst of the Friday afternoon M6 traffic and should get through fairly smoothly.

In many ways, this departure was sadder than when I left my first club where I'd been for five years, rather than these five months here. It was probably due to the acceptance that my dream of managing an Open Championship venue had come to an end.

I remain philosophical, nobody died and nobody got hurt and maybe, just maybe, everyone has learnt a lesson.

I left at lunchtime as planned heading towards my first spell of unemployment since I started work in 1975!

As it happens, on the way back, I receive two calls offering me work!

Firstly, a friend, on behalf of someone else, is manning a stall on the Christmas market selling novelty chocolate tools and he asks if I would like to take some shifts. It is due to run from mid-November until Christmas Eve and obviously I agree. The money won't be great but at least it's some money!

Secondly, the County President of the Leicestershire & Rutland Golf Union calls to see if I would like to take over as County Secretary in February following their Annual General Meeting. The present incumbent is retiring due to ill health and having knowledge about my return to the area following my 'unfortunate' experience, thought of me first. I had no hesitation in accepting and although, payment for that work would only be paid annually, at least, it meant I could stay close to the golf industry in that role and would therefore, hopefully, help me secure further employment in the near future.

Chapter 3

Unemployed

25th October 2014 – 6th April 2015

So, for the first time in my working life, I'm unemployed!!

The first action is to take advantage of a week's holiday with the family on the Norfolk coast. I'd originally planned to just have a long weekend with them but the opportunity arose to have the full week so obviously I took it.

Not only did it give me the chance to unwind, but also provided the opportunity of starting to plan my next moves employment wise.

I'm not the sort of person to just lounge around anyway. I was determined that, once I did get back in front of a prospective employer at a job interviewer, I wasn't going to be in the position of saying that all I'd done is be on the sofa watching Jeremy Kyle and all the other daytime television rubbish.

I planned all the golf-related activities I could still be involved in over the next two to three months.

Of course, I had also got to get my head around selling chocolate tools on the Christmas market so on my return from that week's holiday, I met up with the friend that had called me and got the low down on that role.

Although the pay wasn't great, it was wonderful to do something different and certainly not having the responsibility I'd had in my previous positions was a welcome break. I even used to cycle into town so I got some exercise in and avoided public transport or parking costs.

Responsibility did eventually come my way in this role as the girl appointed as Stall Manager had a row with the organisers and her duties were transferred to me. At least, it meant I received more money as a result of the added responsibility!

The additional duties were no problem, at least not until Christmas Eve. The market ended that day and all stalls had to be cleared ready for their removal on Boxing Day.

The stall had been open until 5.00p.m. and I decided that rather than try and get it emptied at that time, when the city centre was still busy with some people still shopping and some people beginning (or in some cases, continuing) their festive celebrations, I'd return later.

It took three car journeys to remove the stock from the stall to my garage for collection on Boxing Day and just got finished before midnight – it was a race to beat Santa home!

Christmas and the New Year came and went, as did January.

Whilst maintaining my activity in the golf world, the majority of my time was spent supporting the family and did all the domestic chores for a good few weeks.

By the middle of January, two opportunities appeared to open up

Firstly, I received a call informing me that the position at a club just down the road was about to be made vacant and that I should keep an eye out for an advert. Being very familiar with that club, I immediately set to work in recording my knowledge and conducting further research ready for the time of applications arrived.

The advertisement of the vacancy duly arrived and after some minor adjustments to the research I had completed to reflect what they were looking for, I made my application.

Before its fate was known, I received a call one evening as I was about to serve up dinner for the family. In fact, I was at such a crucial stage that I asked my eldest son to answer the phone. He immediately passed it on to me as it was the President of a golf club asking if I would go and work for him if the job at his club became available! The Chairman of my first club had recommended me to him, hence his call to me.

I don't think I need to go into any great detail as to what my response was! It was left that I would send him the information I had sent to apply for the job down the road and he asked me to keep him posted on my progress with that application.

Progress was good, not only had I been successful in achieving an interview, but also I'd found out that only four were being interviewed.

I was as ready as I ever was for that interview. I had arrived in good time and was on the ball for them. The interview went exceptionally well and think it was the best I'd had anywhere and certainly my performance reflected the in depth preparation I'd completed beforehand.

A week later, I received the devastating news that I'd been unsuccessful! It was one of the moments where I can remember where I was at the time I got that news!

Despite my disappointment, I did have the wherewithal to ask for a further meeting to get some feedback and saw two of the selection panel shortly after. My main concern was that my 'unfortunate' experience at the golf club I'd left in October had been held against me but had been assured that if anything, they had appreciated my honesty and my courage in making that decision. I had also been assured that of the four candidates, I had been one of the two that stood out and I had just missed out by a whisker. Close but no cigar!

The President of the club that had contacted me in January but nothing was developing there at that time.

In the meantime, and to ensure some income was coming in, I'd agreed to work for a company that arranges for cars to be delivered all around the country. Basically, you make your way to wherever the car is, collect it and deliver it to where it needs to go, call into the office to get your net assignment and so on and so forth. If you're really lucky, the next car to be collected is at the same destination you've just delivered to. If you're unlucky, it could involve a lengthy hike, buses, trains or taxis. Thumbing a lift wasn't out of the question either but I never had any success in hitch hiking!

The journey I most remember was driving probably the nest car I drove. My first job was to deliver a car to a garage in Hertford and then had to make my way to Purfleet to pick up a new Mercedes E-Class. I tried hitchhiking but without success so in the end, I had to get a train into Liverpool Street and then another out to Purfleet which then left a three mile walk to the collection point. I then had to drive this new Merc around the M25 in rush hour and when it was dark to home where it was kept overnight. The following day, I then had to deliver it to Chesterfield and ater handing it over to its new owner, had to walk two miles to get a bus into Sheffield to collect my next car. It wouldn't have been so bad but the Merc's new owner drove past me whilst I walking for the bus! From the sublime to the ridiculous!

NOTE TO THE READER – if you see someone at the side of the road carrying trade car registration plates, please try and help them out!!

(I'm reminded of a joke here! A hitchhiker is successful in getting a lift. He gets in the passenger seat, thanks the driver for stopping and tells him where he is headed. He says that he thought that no one would pick him up for fear of him being a serial killer. The driver suggests that the odds of two serial killers being in the same car at the same time made that highly unlikely!).

Anyway, the pay wasn't great but it did keep me active and it did offer some flexibility in which to keep my hand in the golf industry.

At some point, I became aware of the successful applicant for the position at the golf club down the road, realised that he come from another club which obviously meant that they now had a vacancy.

I knew a previous incumbent of the role there and I made contact with him only to find that the closing date for that job, which had only been advertised locally, was that day!

I immediately put together an application, updated my Curriculum Vitae and then emailed off to them.

It wasn't long after when I found that I'd had been successful in gaining an interview. There were five on the selection panel but it had obviously gone well as five days later, as I had just got off the train after delivering a car to Lytham St Annes, I was offered the position and I very gratefully accepted.

Immediately!

An interesting golf related interlude during this period of unemployment arose when I was approached by a club to sit on an Appeal Panel with two others.

Basically, a member of their club had been disciplined for an incident that happened on the course and the member had appealed. The club had felt that in order to ensure impartiality, they would arrange for the appeal to be heard by a panel not associated with the club.

The three of us that were to sit on the Appeal Panel were provided copies of all the relevant documentation, together with details of his appeal and arrangements were made to hear that appeal at a neutral venue.

I was elected as Chair of the panel, as well as the note taker and report writer.

On the day of the appeal hearing, the three of us met beforehand to swap notes and agree a strategy for the hearing with the appellant.

The hearing commenced and, to be honest, the Appeal Panel were not presented with any additional evidence or grounds to change the original sanction imposed by the club. However, as the hearing proceeded, it became clear that the appellant was getting more and more agitated of this fact, and I think we all felt that he was en route to exploding – the very issue that had brought him to a Disciplinary Hearing in the first place!

During the questioning by the other two on the panel, I continued to study the information provided regarding the investigation, disciplinary hearing, sanction imposed and the appeal when it suddenly dawned on me that the appeal had been made out of time!!

When the sanction had been imposed, the member was offered the right of appeal and to exercise that right, he had to make it in writing and within fourteen days. His appeal letter was dated outside of that time frame, and we had all missed it in the build up to the hearing!!

This issue was brought to his attention at a suitable juncture in the hearing and he became even more agitated that he couldn't explain why his appeal was out of time.

Anyway, in conclusion the hearing came to an end and the Appeal Panel unanimously agreed that the original sanction imposed by the club should be increased to take account of the delay in the sanction being applied!!

Chapter 4

Elsham Golf Club
Elsham, Lincolnshire

General Manager

7th April 2015 – 18th September 2015

Elsham Golf Club

The club was formed in 1900 and celebrated its centenary in 2000 by being crowned Lincolnshire County Champions.

As you would expect in Lincolnshire, the course is very flat and is a tranquil, well wooded parkland course in a secluded part of the county.

Tony Jacklin played a lot of his golf at Elsham when relaxing away from tournament play following his major wins in the Open Championship in 1969 and US Open in 1970.

In recent years, the club have excelled in looking after the environment on and around the golf course. In addition to award winning special wild flower sites that can be seen in their full glory during the summer months, bird boxes and viewers are installed to further demonstrate their commitment to helping the natural environment.

One of the most significant pieces of their recent history was unfortunately a disaster. A fire that started in the changing room burned down the majority of the clubhouse which meant the loss of vital documents and several items of historical significance.

Monday 7th April 2015

I'm back in the game!! After five months out of golf club management, I start at my new club today.

The downside is that it's a one hundred and twenty five mile round journey from home and I have to navigate twenty two roundabouts to get here!!! Still, at least I'm generally in the quieter direction of traffic.

The irony of this situation, and I do love some irony, is that a few years ago, the manager of the club was the Regional Captain of the East Midlands division of the Golf Club Manager's Association. As a result, one of the regional meetings was held here and I attended it. I can remember commenting at the time at how remote the club was from where I lived and worked – and now I'm going to be going there daily!

I'm not sure why this is significant but I now start work in my third county in golf club management and all of them begin with the letter 'L'! I'm now in Lincolnshire after working in Leicestershire and Lancashire!! Can only think of Lanarkshire now to complete the set?

I'm also on for completing the full set of job titles! I've been Managing Secretary and Business Manager but now I'm the General Manager.

Tuesday 8th April 2015

After yesterday's 'find my feet' day, I can't believe the lack of use of technology to complete even the most simple processes. Just like my previous club, the reliance on hand written books and ledgers is incredible.

I'm not saying I'm the most advanced when it comes to technology, but this will have to change!!

Tony Jacklin's presence looms large throughout the clubhouse!!

Wednesday 9th April 2015

After the usual early start, I pop downstairs to the Gents Changing Room to go to the toilet.

On entering, I encounter around twenty senior members sorting themselves out for their Wednesday morning round.

Not wishing to miss the moment, I ask if it's a bona fide Committee Meeting and should I be there taking notes. This causes some amusement but there are gasps of astonishment with comments along the lines that they couldn't believe that the General Manager was prepared to talk to them. I don't believe my immediate predecessor made too many friends during his short stay here before leaving.

Thursday 16ᵗʰ April 2015

Tonight was my first meeting of the Management Committee at this club – and there's twenty one on the Committee!!

I understand why golf clubs have Committees although I think the structure is a little outdated these days. I think they were ok when clubs were run on a part time, volunteer basis but these days, where full time paid professionals are employed, the need doesn't seem as great but nevertheless, I accepted the role and therefore I have accepted that that's the way it is.

But 21???!!!

There's no wonder these meetings go on all night and hardly anything gets decided.

In my experience, you get twice as much done, in half the time when there are fewer attending these meetings.

Monday 11ᵗʰ May 2015

I've arrived at the golf club as usual and am immediately confronted by the spokesman for a group of travellers that have settled in the car park overnight.

Before I park my car I'm asked if I'm the main man and when I inform them that I'm the General Manager, I'm told that they want £1500.00 to leave! I ask if I could have a few minutes, get parked up, go into the club and tell them I will be back out shortly.

Whilst in the club, in addition to notifying the police, I receive a visit from the Treasurer who had become aware of their visit and he authorises me to negotiate with them up to £1200.00 to go.

I then return to the spokesman of the travellers with the Treasurer in tow. The spokesman asks me if I'm going to pay their fee to leave.

I inform him that I have informed the police about their presence and they will be taking action in due course. I tell him that his offer has been considered but I expressed the concern that if we paid it, they would merely pack up, move down the road and then return to try and obtain a further payment. Equally, I also suggested that having received our money for them to leave, they might contact their fellow travellers to tell them that we were a soft touch and would therefore get visits from them as well. I said that seeing as we haven't got lots of £1500.00's to give away, I may as well start by saying no to them from the outset.

With that I asked them to leave and within two hours, they did!!

I think we were very lucky with this one. I know that many golf clubs have been used as temporary homes for these travellers and some have caused many problems for those clubs.

As it turned out, we only have three caravans, they had left within twenty-four hours of their arrival, and they even bagged up their rubbish before leaving – I think that's what they call a result!

Saturday 27th June 2015

It's Captain's Day today and at this club, the manager is expected to play a part and so I'm at work. However, it did present a first last night – I slept overnight in the Greenkeeper's Sheds!

I'd got to be back at work early this morning and therefore, I really didn't want to have to face the Friday evening rush hour traffic, to get home late, only to return early this morning. Not to mention the cost of fuel!

So on Thursday, I'd been down to the sheds to have a look and found that the room where the team relax during their breaks could easily accommodate me, particularly as it was my intention to take one of our camping beds, pillows and sleeping bags to get down on. I'd even got a bed side light to read! Security was no problem as I could lock the sheds from the inside and that was still preferable than the clubhouse where the alarm would have to remain unset for the night.

My greatest fear for the night was rats but I didn't hear or see any – fortunately!

Wednesday 1st July 2015

In the introduction for Elsham Golf Club, I mentioned that they'd previously had a fire that caused considerable damage to the clubhouse. Well we've had another disaster today!!

There's been a storm and lightning has struck our irrigation system which has put part of the system out of action but more importantly, it's going to cost over £30000 to put it right!!

Friday 3rd July 2015

Now I have long been an enthusiastic advocate of POETS Day – 'Piss Off Early, Tomorrow is Saturday'! (Apologies for the swearing Mum!). Even in the days when I was at the Bank and the branch was open until 6.00pm, I was long gone by closing time!

So given that background, it doesn't please me greatly when a meeting is called for 5.00 p.m. this evening to discuss where we are in relation to making an application for grant to install new practice facilities and a short game area. Nevertheless, of course, it never entered my head not to be there – that's the job!

Ten people, including myself, were to attend this meeting, but by the time 5.15 p.m. had arrived, the only people there were the Captain, Ladies Captain (they were husband and wife) and myself! After a further fifteen minutes, and still no one arriving, the Captain decided to postpone the meeting!!! Clearly everyone else shared my view of POETS Day!!

I'm not a happy bunny as I drive the sixty-two and a half miles home, on a Friday night in rush hour traffic.

Thursday 9th July 2015

My day started off at the first golf club I'd worked at as it's my Assistant's birthday tomorrow, so I called in to see her and take a card and present.

On the journey back to my current club, I received a call on my mobile but as I'm without a hands-free kit, I do not take it but a message has been left.

On arrival at work, I am immediately thrown into the day's activities and do not have the opportunity to access that message until later. It turns out to be from a former member of that first club. In the intervening time, he moved to another club and subsequently became their Treasurer. He explained that the club are re-structuring and would like to speak to me about the possibility of going to work there.

The club in question is much nearer home and after the debacle of last Friday's meeting, if I can say that seeing as no meeting was actually held, I agree to meet them.

Thursday 13th August 2015

One of the things that all of those that are involved with the game of golf love is the tradition and history that goes with the game and last night's function was a prime example.

It was the annual dinner for all of the surviving Past Captain's to attend and last night, they all did. Basically, it's nothing more than a dinner with a few speeches thrown in but at the end of it, they all take wine and toast the club.

The thing here is that they take wine from a quaich, a shallow, two handled drinking cup that originated in Scotland and it must be more than a coincidence that that's where the game also originated. Unless of course you're Dutch, in which case, you believe that the game of golf began there).

When this 'ritual' began, each Past Captain had their own quaich, which had been engraved with their name and the year of their captaincy. However, during the intervening time, this had stalled due to the failure to obtain a further supply of quaiches. For this year's event, we have some Past Captain's without quaiches, but we also have some quaiches that belonged to Past Captains that had passed away.

I took on the job of trying to find similar quaiches to rectify this situation, but like all of my predecessors, failed. However, in order to ensure that all current Past Captains have a quaich for this year's event, I suggested that their names be engraved on those that had previously belonged to a Past Captain. This would also mean that their place in history would be preserved. In view of the reaction to my suggestion, you would have thought that I had come up with the Theory of Relativity or the Meaning of Life! It was very enthusiastically taken up.

Thursday 20th August 2015

Tonight's meeting of the Management Committee got off to late start as I was called down to the Gents toilets – a blockage had caused a flood and I spent an hour with mop and bucket clearing up the mess! Nothing to do with golf!!!

Wednesday 2nd September 2015

I've had a meeting with a member today – a meeting that I called.

I wanted to speak to him about his behaviour on the golf course. There have been repeated incidents where he had been known to demonstrate his frustration at the game by throwing clubs, swearing and by leaving the golf course without completing the eighteen holes. He's even been known to 'Nil Return' (See below) on the first hole and walk off the course!!

His behaviour is clearly detrimental to his game and membership, those he is playing with and also breaches the etiquette of the game.

Apparently, this has been going on for a number of years but no one has ever said anything to him. I understood that he was a former boxer so whether or not that's the reason he's not been spoken to, I'm not sure, but I'm certainly not shirking the responsibility.

I explained to him that we are in the leisure industry and that when players arrive at the club and move on to the first tee, I expect them to have the opportunity of enjoying their morning or afternoon with us rather than have to put up with his anti-social antics! I have also explained that, having played the game for forty years, I entirely accept that it is a frustrating game but if he can't get over that, then he needs to find a new sport.

He accepted that he has anger management issues and that he is trying to deal with them.

I informed him that I am no longer prepared to accept his behaviour and that if there are any further issues, then he would leave me with no alternative but to cancel his membership with immediate effect.

Note - Nil Return is the technical term for a player failing to record a score over the eighteen holes.

Friday 18th September 2015

My last day here!! This is becoming a bad habit!!

Having spent twenty-two years at TSB Bank, I've now had four jobs in the last year and had a period of unemployment!!

Earlier in the year, I had received a telephone call from someone at Kirby Muxloe Golf Club asking if I would be prepared to work with him there. At that time, I was unemployed following my spell at West Lancs and of course, I said I would.

However, the trail went cold from there until we got to July when I received a call from a former member of Lingdale. He had moved to another club and was in an Officer position and he informed me that his current club were very interested in employing me to carry out a restructure.

Of course, I was very interested and did meet with them. All was progressing well but then the recruitment process slowed. In the meantime, the guy at Kirby got wind of this other interest and, to cut a long story short, they got to the line first.

I was made an attractive offer and not just because it didn't involve that one hundred- and twenty-five-mile journey to get to work!

My last day was uneventful and there was no leaving 'do' as such although I did visit all the staff before I left.

Chapter 5

Kirby Muxloe Golf Club
Kirby Muxloe, Leicestershire

Club Manager

21st September 2015 - Present

Kirby Muxloe Golf Club

Formed in 1893 and like the West Lancashire Golf Club, it owed its formation to the development of the railway. The building of rail links to outlying villages from the city of Leicester provided much needed transport for city dwellers and the golf course was the brainchild of businessmen from the village.

Again, like many clubs, its existence began as a nine hole course but in 1927, it was decided to extend it to eighteen holes. This meant that a major part of the original course was abandoned.

One of the first Presidents of the club was Alderman E. Wood. He later became Mayor of Leicester (1907) and was known as the founder of Freeman, Hardy & Willis, the shoe manufacturing company.

Like many similar long-standing clubs, it has celebrated its centenary and more recent, its quasquicentennial (125 years).

One of the most talked about events was when the World Cup winning squad, including Manager Sir Alf Ramsey, arrived for golf in March 1984 when current member Gordon Banks invited his old teammates to join him.

2016 saw a significant step in the club's history when it hosted the English Senior Men's Open Amateur Strokeplay Championship, the biggest competition that the club had held since its formation.

KIRBY MUXLOE GOLF CLUB

Monday 21st September 2015

Day 1 at my new club and you'll never guess what? Not only am I in a county beginning with 'L' – I'm back in Leicestershire (not Lanarkshire) - but I have a new job title, I'm the Club Manager at this Kirby Muxloe.

This morning saw me meet with the President who gave me a little more background on the club and that included a buggy ride around the course which I assume would be similar to a white-knuckle ride at Alton Towers!! I say assume as I don't usually go on them!

As we go around the course, I meet up with one of the greenkeepers that used to work at my first club before moving on to this one. After a little conversation, I ask him where I could find the Head Greenkeeper so that we could have an initial meet and introduction. As it happens, I knew this guy as he was interviewed at my first club for the same position there but he obviously failed to secure that appointment. The reason he didn't get it was that the successful candidate was head and shoulders above the remainder of those that were interviewed although he didn't help himself when, during a presentation that was part of the recruitment process, he accused the current team of lazy greenkeeping. This didn't go down too well with the former Chair of the Greens Committee, who was in attendance on the panel, and he took an instant dislike.

Anyway, having asked the question as to where he was, I got a sheepish response that he wasn't around, and I immediately suspected that this matter goes deeper than that.

Friday 27th November 2015

As at my previous club, I begin the issue of a weekly newsletter to members.

There have been a few 'prototypes' prior to this but Issue No.1 goes out today.

Monday 14th December 2015

Mondays are generally very quiet around here, so quiet in fact that the bar is only open for a short period and the kitchen isn't even open at all.

Friday 22nd January 2016

Today was one of those occasions when I was somewhere I shouldn't have been and really wish I had have been where I should have been!

I was supposed to be attending a meeting of the Golf Club Manager's Association, and whilst it was my intention to join that meeting late, I had to go into work first thing

At last night's meeting of Council, they had decided that the contract of employment of the Head Greenkeeper should be terminated with immediate effect. The President, Captain and I would deliver the news to him first thing the following morning i.e. this morning.

I won't go into detail here but suffice to say, it didn't go well!

In fact, this was probably the worst day of my golf club management career, if not the worst day in my work career to date!

Friday 22nd January 2016

After the trauma of the events first thing and having attended the Golf Club Manager's Association meeting, I returned to work.

Despite the unsavoury event of the morning. I had to be the life and soul of the party by hosting a Race Night at the club! I did manage to carry it off and the evening went well.

Wednesday 9th March 2016

When I first started at this club, there was already an ongoing saga of a claim from a member who had been relocated by his employer one hundred and thirty miles away. The member had asked for a partial refund on his subscription seeing as he could no longer play for the remainder of that year.

The club steadfastly refused to allow the refund in the interests of other members, but the guy was undeterred and consistently wrote to the club about it – in fact it must have cost more to keep responding that it would have done to make the requested refund!

Today was going to be the day that this matter got resolved. I'd been at the club for six months and it had been going on before my arrival.

The member had taken the club to the Small Claims Court but before the case was heard, they wanted it to go to mediation and that was set for this morning.

The committee had tasked me with dealing with the matter on the club's behalf with the mandate to do whatever was necessary to make the matter go away! Possibly a wrong move on their part as I had some sympathy with the guy. My take on the matter was that he hadn't changed his mind about his membership, he hadn't decided to switch his membership to a rival club up the road, he'd simply been the 'victim' of his employer's requirement of re-deploying him elsewhere in the country!

Anyway, down to the mediation process. I was called by the mediator who explained the process. Basically, he would call me to see if I was prepared to budge. He would then ring the member to see if he would budge and so on and so forth. I was first up offering a refund of £50.00 and by the end of this process, guess what? We ended up halfway between what he wanted as a refund and what we wanted to give us a refund!

What a farce and a complete waste of time!

Thursday 17th March 2016

Today was entirely spent attending a First Aid workshop with the Greens Team.

Thursday 31st March 2016

Attended a Safeguarding & Child Protection workshop this evening at a nearby club.

Tuesday 31st May 2016

You'll have seen from my diary entry in July 2014, that it is a great honour when some of the game's leading lights come to visit and today is no exception.

We're hosting England Golf's Senior Men's Open Amateur Championship this week, today is the second practice day before the competition begins tomorrow.

One of the competitors happens to be none other than the Chief Executive of the Royal & Ancient Golf Club of St Andrews!

Of course, this presents another 1st Tee photo opportunity which doesn't go begging and I make the most of a little career enhancing 'sucking up' by reserving a car park space especially for him during his stay with us.

As it happens, I never saw him again that week!

Friday 17th July 2016

Golf courses are very popular for scattering the ashes of the recently departed. I assume families would like their ashes scattered where they spent much of their spare leisure time with their friends and fellow members.

The usual procedure for such ceremonies would be for me to make arrangements for them to attend the club and establish where they would like the ashes to be scattered. When they arrive, I would then either walk or transport them out to the chosen area, depending on how far away it is from the clubhouse. On arrival at that chosen location, I would then leave the family to give them some privacy and allow them to have their own 'service' before the scattering.

Over the years, it has never failed to surprise me on how few take into account any breeze (there's usually some around on a wide open golf course) there is and end up with some of the ashes of the recently departed blowing all over the 'scatterer'.

Anyway, today's event was slightly different. The ashes were contained in a glass bottle and the family wanted them in the bunker on the tenth hole. I drove them out there and then left them alone to conduct their service. I was some two hundred yards away but could see that rather than scattering the ashes, they merely buried them, still in the glass bottle, in the bunker.

Once the service was over, they called me and I transported them back to the clubhouse. They returned to their car and then drove off.

Now obviously, there was a real issue here. I could a golfer's ball entering the bunker at the exact same spot and when they played their recovery shot, glass would explode everywhere following the impact of the club.

I couldn't leave in there, so I returned to the bunker, retrieved the glass bottle, scattered the ashes and then put the glass bottle in our recycling bin.

Monday 8th August 2016

News has filtered through that the Harley Staples Cancer Trust have finally got the keys to Harley's House situated in Rutland, just minutes from Rutland Water. Families who have a child battling with cancer are welcome to take a free holiday for up to a week. This will give the family a chance to relax and escape from hospitals and spend quality family time together creating memories to cherish forever.

It is very rewarding to know that I played, even if just a small part, in the opening of Harley's House.

Monday 26th September 2016

My youngest son started work as an Accountant some months ago and the firm had decided that to celebrate its 70th

Anniversary by holding a golf day and, through his influence, it was being held here.

I had a week's holiday booked in Lanzarote but quickly changed arrangements when I realised there was a clash as I wanted to be here to ensure everything went smoothly for him and for them. And it did!

I tried as much as I could to make it as difficult as possible for him to win the Longest Drive competition but sadly ailed as he won it by a country mile.

To end this diary entry, I cannot resist mentioning that this event clashed with Bryan Ferry's birthday although he was a year older than the accountancy firm!

Wednesday 26th October 2016

As a result of the events of January earlier this year, we recruited a new Head Greenkeeper and he started with us in April, and in line with his pedigree, the course, in a short space of time, had improved drastically according to the majority of members.

There had been some calls to parade him to the membership and therefore I arranged a 'social' for tonight – 'An Evening with the Head Greenkeeper'.

Now I'll admit straight away that I organised it for one of the quieter nights of the week in the clubhouse in order to drum up some additional bar trade. In the event, almost one hundred members attended.

The format of the evening was for him to give a presentation on the current condition of the golf course and where he sees it going over the next few years, have an interval (get the bar till ringing) and then hold a Question & Answer session.

The first part of the evening had gone well and for the second part, I acted as Master of Ceremonies to offer some support to the Head Greenkeeper.

The evening went very well but there was one question that I wouldn't allow him to answer as there were political connotations!

He was asked about what he thought about the size of the Greens Committee. I reminded that the questioner that all of us that work in golf clubs accept that we have to work with Committees and Sub Committees. I also reminded him that we also accept that members had elected the Chair of the Committee and that Council had approved the composition of the Committee when asked to do so shortly after the Annual General Meeting. It was therefore not appropriate for us to comment on the suitability or size of any Committee to which I received a resounding round of applause.

Friday 20th January 2017

It's the Winter Meeting of the East Midlands Region of the Golf Club Managers' Association today and following a request from the Regional Secretary, I have volunteered to go to Birmingham Airport to pick up one of the leading lights in

Europe on the subject of managing a golf club. He's Dutch and flying in from the Netherlands.

The travel to the airport is fine but negotiating the car park proves difficult – especially that post that came from nowhere is smash by rear passenger stop light!!

That aside, the collection of our guest goes smoothly and it's not long before we're in the car and headed to the meeting venue.

What I'd not realised or anticipated was that I would get a grilling during the journey on the way about the club I'm based at and the way I manage!

Arrival at the meeting couldn't come soon enough!

Wednesday 12th April 2017

The last job I do before leaving the office each evening is to see what's on for the following day both in the club diary and in my own diary to ensure I'm ready when I arrive the following morning.

On arrival, the first job is then to check emails and telephone messages to see if there is anything that has happened that might have changes things.

Given the above, and after identifying that there were no functions on today, you can imagine my surprise to be disturbed mid-morning by an elderly lady who has arrived for the meeting!

Of course, the first reaction is to think what's gone wrong and then to check diaries and calendars etc but still I couldn't find her meeting.

After further discussion with her, I found out that she was a week early! And she had driven one hundred miles!!

Before she turned round to make the journey home, I made sure she had a rest and provided a drink and sandwich.

Wednesday 19th April 2017

The elderly lady that last Wednesday came a week early for her meeting has now arrived safely for the scheduled time and date.

Of course, I didn't say anything to her that would cause embarrassment amongst her colleagues - although I did say how nice it was to see her again!

Thursday 15th June 2017

Last Saturday, we hosted an evening function for one of our members whose wife was celebrating a significant birthday.

It's taken us until today to finally remove all the fake tan from the toilet seats in the Ladies changing room!

Tuesday 5th September 2017

In this day and age, you can't refer to Tuesdays as Ladies Day, but nevertheless, the vast majority of Ladies do play on that day. However, they no longer enjoy exclusive rights over the course and men do play outside of the periods that the Ladies do.

Many of the more senior Ladies, whose playing days are behind them, also still visit on a Tuesday and have lunch with their friends so its quite a social day at the club.

One of the more elderly ladies, who still travels to the club by car, has visited me in the office to say that she has a problem.

When parking her car, she has misjudged the distance to the kerb, done over it and now her car is 'trapped' by the kerb as she can't reverse back over it.

I've been out to have a go but without any success so there was only one other thing to do – I contacted the Greenkeeping team to all come over to the clubhouse in the hope that we could lift the car sufficiently to get it back over the kerb.

Fortunately, with a little manoeuvring, we managed to get it free! I've asked her to park in one of the central spaces in future!

Monday 11th September 2017

My weekly newsletter has been very useful in relaying messages to the membership and often at management meetings, I'm asked to include a topic.

Today, I've received a call from a member of management asking me to make mention of something in this week's edition and I ask "Whatever did you do before the newsletter?"

"Kept it a secret" is his response!

Wednesday 26th October 2017

The Bar Surpervisor has been in to see me about the recent stocktake of the bar and the resultant report.

It had come to light that just before the Stocktaker's visit, one of the bar staff had borrowed a bottle of champagne had not replaced it until after the report but it being missing had not been noted on the report. It should be said that our champagne sales are not great and therefore a missing bottle should have stood out.

I contacted the Stocktaker about this issue and he informed me that he had noted the bottle being missing, didn't report it (for some nebulous reason) but then forgot to make mention of it in his summary.

Given that the sole purpose of his visit is to count what stock we have and report it and that clearly he had failed to do that, I have begun the search for a new stocktaker!

Wednesday 7th December 2017

It's another car park tale for today!

One of the senior members of the club has turned up for their Wednesday roll up but before his arrival at the club, he's taken his car into a garage for a service and while they do it, they've loaned him a courtesy car.

He's parked up in one of the upper central spaces that is slightly downhill. When he returned after golf, someone has parked in the opposite lower space i.e. uphill, and only about two inches from his loan car.

He came to see me because, as he was unfamiliar with the loan car, he was reluctant to try and move it for fear of rolling into the other car!

I've therefore had to go out, get the car started and then rev it up in reverse before releasing the handbrake and get him out of his predicament!

Just doing my job sir!

Monday 18ᵗʰ December 2017

During the summer, there was an unsavoury incident at the club that could not be proved one way or another and therefore no action could be taken. The main reason for this was that although we had CCTV installed, it did not record and so was only of any use if the screen was being viewed at the time.

In view of this, I managed to convince Council to stump up the funds to install a new system and they agreed. The new system, with record and playback facilities was out in but, crucially, we didn't tell anyone about it!

I've come into work this morning on a mission! Yesterday, I was informed that whilst attending the Christmas Party on Saturday night, a member had his car stolen, although it was subsequently found behind a hedge near the Professional's Shop the following morning. The incident had been reported to the police and the member and his wife had, quite understandably, spent an uncomfortable and sleepless Saturday night.

My job this morning was to review the CCTV footage to try and establish, if possible, what had happened.

The footage showed that two members, that weren't attending the Christmas Party, had left the clubhouse, albeit not together. One was seen in the area where the stolen car was parked and was then seen coming from where the car ended up. The other was seen approaching the stolen car before it was moved and then seen returning the clubhouse whilst it was en route to its resting place. Both were then seen returning into the clubhouse for a short while before leaving for the evening.

From speaking to the owner of the car, he had left the keys in his overcoat in the changing room before attending the dinner.

Whilst discussions were ongoing with officers of the club, it was decided that the two 'suspects' would be suspended from the club while the investigation was ongoing.

One of the two 'suspects' called me and asked for a meeting, which I agreed to, and when he arrived, the other was in tow and I agreed to see them together, in the company of a member of Council that was in the clubhouse at the time.

Prior to their arrival, I had taken some still photographs from the CCTV footage to evidence what I had seen and their faces themselves were a picture as it dawned on them that the CCTV had recorded the events as they unfolded that evening.

The upshot of this incident was that the police decided not to take any action but both of the 'suspects' remained suspended until the end of the subscription year and they were not invited to renew their membership.

Tuesday 19th December 2017

Today is the monthly meeting of the House Committee although the diary entry really begins on Saturday 9th December 2017.

On that evening, it snowed and it snowed and it snowed!! And continued to do so well into Sunday!!

I managed to get out from home during the Sunday morning in order to make the weekly visit to see my mother albeit very carefully. Once out on to the main roads, they were not good but passable with care.

I reached the supermarket across the road from where she lives, made the usual phone call to her to tell here where I was and ask if there was any other shopping she wanted doing other than getting her newspaper.

While in the supermarket, I received a telephone call from the bar person on duty that day and she was expressing great concern about the road situation and making it clear that she would rather not have to make that journey.

Obviously, taking into account the welfare and safety of staff and also the fact that we were unlikely to be very busy (!), I telephoned the President and recommended that we should close the clubhouse for the day – while we have a no closure policy for the golf course, seeing as there would have been six inches of snow on the ground, it was extremely unlikely that anyone would be playing today.

He entirely agreed with my recommendation and therefore, I contacted all the staff due in that day to tell them not to make the journey and when I arrived at mothers, I sent a message to all members about the decision via my phone and amended the website to provide further information.

I had assured the President that I would go into work the following morning to assess conditions and when I arrived, they had got worse if anything and so I made further contact with the President and as a result, we remained closed for that day and also the following two days. Although the snow thawed, it was very cold and the car park was like a sheet of ice and not safe at all.

I continued to go into work each day to assess conditions, check pipes and security and of course, I could continue to keep on top of phone messages and emails. I also provided a daily report to members, with photographic evidence, of the position at the club.

By the time, Wednesday afternoon came, we made the decision to re-open the following day and although we weren't busy, at least we were back in the game.

At the start of the following week, the bar person that had contacted me on the Sunday morning started to make protestations that she wasn't going to get paid during those four days of closure as she was on a zero hours contract. (Remember, that she started the process that led to the closure by her call to me on the Sunday).

I realise that there are mixed views about such contracts but they do provide benefits for both employer and employee in that there are not so many ties and there is a greater degree of flexibility for both parties. The employee after all still receives pay, payment in lieu of holiday entitlement, pension contributions, in fact all the benefits of an employee that is not on a zero hours contract.

As a result of her protestations, discussions were being held with the officers of the club about this situation and she was aware that these were ongoing. However, they had not been concluded by the time we arrived at this meeting of the House Committee and she was attending as the representative for the bar.

Once we received the 'Bar' item on the agenda, she took the opportunity of continuing her protest but obviously to the wider audience that this committee provided. I suggested that the forum of the committee was not the appropriate place to discuss personal job contracts and assured her that discussions were underway outside of this meeting to look at this matter. Despite the Chair of the Committee, the President and the Vice President being in attendance and failing to intervene, she continued to voice her protest and at one point, looked at me and said that I would still get paid for those days.

I immediately reminded her that I went to work and therefore I don't see why I shouldn't get paid!

There was no further discussion on this matter at this meeting!

Friday 10th January 2018

The latest copy of The Golf Club Manager, the monthly magazine of the Golf Club Managers' Association (GCMA) has dropped through the letterbox this morning and I have a particular interest in it this month – I'm featured in it (on Pages 64 & 65) for the article "A week in the life of…"!

Whilst at the recent GCMA Conference, I was approached to see if I would be interested in participating and, obviously, I said yes! Not sure if they were so desperate for copy that they asked me or that, as I'm a previous Runner Up in their Golf Club Manager of the Year competition, they thought I might be an interesting subject!!

The basic premise of the article is write to write about your week and whilst I included many issues to do with work and how it is planned, I also managed to get some personal references in included my granddaughter, knitting (you'll have to read the piece!), baking mince pies, Nottingham Forest and my relationship with the Friday Girls (which included a picture with them).

An interesting departure from the usual day job!

Sunday 25th March 2018

It's my birthday today and the R&A's marketing machine is in full working order:-

Tuesday 24th April 2018

Even on holiday, golf is never far away as I walk from Santa Eulalia to Ibiza Town!!

Friday 25th May 2018

Yippee! Some new legislation comes into force today – the General Data Protection Regulations (GDPR).

Basically this involves all companies adopting a Privacy Policy, obtaining consent for any personal information held and having authority to send marketing information out.

Now call me an old cynic but I really don't think that golf clubs have ever had a breach of confidentiality or in abusing information held on either its members or its visitors. I'm sure that this legislation is aimed at larger companies who have been guilty of those charges but nevertheless, we still have to comply.

Whilst it was a bit of a pain in getting the consent from members and having to delete marketing databases, the main issue for me was that the distribution list for my weekly newsletter reduced by over two hundred names as I couldn't get the necessary authority from members.

Of course, the other outcome was the complaints from members that had not provided consent asking why I had stopped sending them the newsletter!

Thursday 7th June 2018

The golf club I'm working at own a bungalow on the drive that leads to the main car park, clubhouse and course.

A situation has developed where the roots of a tree at the entrance of their drive are starting to cause a problem with the drive and therefore, we have called in a tree surgeon to remove the tree and today's the day.

Around lunchtime, I have to leave to make a brief visit to another golf club and whilst, I leave the club, I pull up to speak to him and see how it is going. Everything was fine and clearly, he knew what he was doing and was making it look very easy and was keeping everything tidy.

As I got back in my car, I remembered that two weeks ago, I moved home and in the new place, there's a wood burning stove. I got back out of my car, had a word, and by the time I returned, I was able to fill my boot with logs ready to keep the house warm during the winter.

Monday 11th June 2018

We've recently taken on a young man as a new Apprentice Greenkeeper.

The Head Greenkeeper and I had met with him for an interview and during that meeting, we had done our best to point out all of the downsides of the job – early mornings, weekend working, cold and wet outdoor working etc. Obviously we didn't want to talk him out of it but we wanted to make sure he was aware that it wasn't all being out in the sunshine and playing golf.

Anyway, he wasn't deterred and accepted the position.

Now don't get me wrong, some of these so called 'millennials' are excellent workers who make an excellent contribution. Others appear to be more focussed on attending to their mobile phones which at times appear to be surgically attached.

Unfortunately, our young man fell into the latter category and whilst out on a buggy today, but watching his phone rather than the way ahead, didn't see the ditch approaching and promptly drove into it!

There are lots of health and safety issues on golf courses and we need people out there who are focussed on what they are doing rather than their phone. As a result of this matter, we had to take the decision to part company and suggested to him that he find something he was going to be more interested in.

Friday 6ᵗʰ July 2018

This week, we have been hosting England Golf for their Women's Open Matchplay Championship where the best lady golfers in country assemble to compete for the title. It's a long week with long days but it is a tremendous honour and privilege to host such events.

In addition to fulfilling my day job, I also have many other roles to complete this week, not only in assisting England Golf and but also in supporting the other team members at the club.

During the first two days of the event, I have observed a gentleman riding around the course in an official England Golf buggy and therefore thought no more about it. However, as we were closing down for the day last night, it came to my attention that not only is he not a member of the official party (it hasn't been satisfactorily explained why he's using an official buggy to get around the course) but also that he has been guilty of getting a little too close to some of the young ladies who are wearing golf attire to reflect the very hot summer that we've been enjoying.

I've asked to be kept informed of this issue today and whilst I was performing score recording duties on the tenth tee, I heard via the walkie talkie system that this guy had arrived for that day's play. A little time after, the England Golf representative came over the radio requesting assistance from a referee to deal with him. Having heard this, I radioed to say that I would deal with it and started to make my way from the tenth tee towards the clubhouse.

On arrival, I introduced myself offered my hand for a handshake. The gentlemen declined to give me his name, declined the handshake but offered a fistbump! I declined and asked his name and what his business was at this event. He declined to answer both. I asked him again and once again he failed to provide the information requested.

As a result, I asked that he immediately leave the clubhouse and all surrounds of the golf club. He asked if he could stay for something to eat and I repeated that I required him to leave immediately. At that point, he turned and headed to the car park. During that walk, he did stop and asked me my name and position and I answered both questions before he resumed his walk to the car park. I followed him and then watched him get in his car and then drive off.

I told all involved that I should be immediately informed if and when he returns (he didn't!).

Amongst all the many roles I have performed as a golf club manager, this was the first time I had been a bouncer!!

Saturday 7th July 2018

I'm at work today because the semi-finals and final of the English Women's Open MatchPlay Championship are being played here.

The competition has gone well and the hot, sunny summer has continued for us.

There's just one small obstacle to overcome on this final afternoon, England are playing in the World Cup quarter final and the second half is likely to impact on the Ladies final, particularly if the football goes to extra time and penalties.

Earlier, this year, we had refurbished our 19th Bar which included redecoration, new furniture, the removal of a snooker table with a pool table coming in its place and two additional large screen televisions which meant that there are now four in total in the clubhouse.

These facilities have been well patronised over the past few weeks as England have progressed in the competition. Today was no exception and by the time kick off came around, the lounge was full. The only problem is that the noise from the televisions is not exactly synchronised so when there was a goal (there were two today) and any sort of close call, there would be a Mexican wave of noise going through the clubhouse.

Fortunately, the match ended in normal time, with a victory for England, and the presentation was only delayed for a few minutes. It had been decided to delay so that the presentation would not be interrupted and members would be around to support it.

Saturday 21st July 2018

Following their kind 'invitation' to join the R&A at Carnoustie for the 147th playing of The Open, I'm here!

Friday 3rd August 2018

We holding our Senior Mixed Open next Wednesday and I have received a telephone request from one of the teams of four asking if they can use the car park overnight to camp in their mobile home. They're from south of the club but are having a few days in the Lake District before calling in for our competition on the way home.

Despite my previous experiences with caravanners and travellers, their story checks out and I'm happy to agree.

Thursday 30th August 2018

Catering is an issue at most golf clubs, I know from my experience at four clubs and any club that has satisfactory arrangements are well advised to maintain them, regardless of whether it is an in-house operation or franchised out.

At the start of this year, the club recognised that, for the large part during the week, we do not need a qualified chef to provide the basic food requirements of either our members or visitors to the club. With that in mind, the decision was taken to operate with two cooks during the week and then outsource function catering to a more qualified caterer.

Today, we have a visiting golf party of seventy-two golfers that require bacon rolls and tea/coffee before play at 11.00am and then a two course dinner after play. We therefore decide that the bacon rolls can be provided in house and then the after-play dinner can be outsourced.

Then came the problem!

One of the cooks had been off sick for some time with some serious non work related issues but nevertheless, the second cook was more than capable of providing the before play food requirements – had she have turned up for work!

Earlier in the year, I had agreed to undertake Basic Food Hygiene training, as well as training on some of the cooking appliances in order to provide bacon rolls to early starting parties to save bringing in cooks to do it. No problem – I'm happy to muck in where necessary and also more than happy to support any of the team.

It had got to around 10.00am on this particular day and in order to ensure we were prepared for the seventy two when they started arriving, I went into the kitchen to start preparing plates and napkins.

At 10.30am, and with no sight or sound from the cook due to be on duty, I start preparing the rolls by cutting and buttering them.

By 10.45am, and still no sign, I unpack the bacon and start laying them out on trays ready to go in the oven. I get through half of them and get them in the oven to start cooking, while continuing to lay out the remaining bacon on more trays.

With the help from one of the bar staff, we managed to get all seventy rolls out and without too much of a delay and get the golfers out on the course without any undue delay.

Once that had been completed, I went to the office to check emails on the club landline and on my personal mobile but nothing. I tried calling her but only got an invitation to leave a voicemail – which I did and by the time I left in the evening, I had still not received a message to explain her absence. I didn't hear from her the day after either!

I can assure the reader, that whilst regrettable, that young lady's career with us did not last for much longer after this episode.

Wednesday 12th September 2018

Today, we're hosting the Autumn Meeting of the East Midlands Region of the Golf Club Manager's Association.

The day involves a business meeting in the morning, followed by a light lunch, golf and then a two-course dinner.

I'd been suffering from a cold and this morning was feeling particularly off. In fact, had this meeting been held anywhere else, I would have cried off and there was a distinct possibility that I wouldn't have gone to work at all.

(Note: I believe that my attendance record at work has been excellent. Yes, I did have a blip in 1997 when I ended up having five months off work following contracting pneumonia but otherwise, my attendance record has been sound).

Anyway, I did attend and after announcing a welcome from the club and pointing out the various housekeeping arrangements, I informed the meeting that despite feeling under the weather, I was still going to take part in the afternoon's golf and that would be a first for me. I did however state that due to my cold, I expected to have to take a dope test, given all the performance enhancing drugs I was taking. Today's format is common for these meetings but I've always left once the business element has concluded in order to return to work.

It was a very pleasant day and I think that, as I had no expectation for doing well in the golf, I was very relaxed, took it easy and just got through as best I could.

Well knock me down with a feather, I only went and won it and by some considerable distance too! My first individual golf win since 1984!! In my winner's speech, amongst other comments, I thanked my sponsors for the day – Nurofen, Strepsils, Beechams and Kleenex!!

Collecting the trophy from the Regional Secretary.

Friday 26th October 2018

Here's a first for me!

As we now have many non-members coming along for lunch on a Sunday, I'm asked to put notices up to direct parents to the disabled toilet which includes nappy changing facilities!

Tuesday 8th January 2019

At this time of year, most suppliers of beer, spirits etc have announced that their prices are increasing, and this year is no different.

Prices are increasing by 5% and we have decided to pass these increases on so I have someone working on updating them on the till ready for business opening.

While doing this, I'm asked if we should also apply the increases to bar snacks, particularly as we have not amended those prices for some time.

After giving the matter some thought, I suggest that we should leave them as they are. These price increases are as a result of the supplier increasing theirs and as we buy bar snacks from a separate source, we would have some difficulty in justifying their increase.

I add "Anyway, it's only peanuts!!"

BOOM! BOOM!!

Thursday 24th January 2019

A free magazine is distributed to golf clubs on a monthly basis and today's carries a headline of "Why it's time to ditch golf club committees".

No comment!

Having said that, I like it would be appropriate to add that I have recently completed reading a series of twenty-two paperbacks which all contain a central character – 'our hero'. In one of them, he has to undertake some surveillance on the 'baddie' and to do that, an allied force has broken into a bowls club across the road and changed the locks. Our hero asks what happens when the people from the bowls club come back. He's told that by the time the committee have had a meeting to establish what has happened, then had another meeting to see what they are going to do about it, and then had another meeting to see how they are going to finance the repairs and new locks, our hero would be long gone!

Monday 21st January 2019

Found an anomaly in our accounting procedures!

One of the younger bar staff had asked if he could offer cocktails at the function on Saturday evening. This of course was warmly welcomed and his initiative and enthusiasm was applauded.

The ingredients for his concoctions were purchased and his drinks priced accordingly.

On arrival at the club this morning, I looked on the records to find out how cocktail sales had gone to find no record of any!

When further enquiries were made later in the day once the bar staff had arrived, I found that as he couldn't locate the appropriate button on the till, he had recorded the £6.00 sales as six £1.00 burger toppings!!

Wednesday 30th January 2019

We've been having a problem with the roof of our walk-in fridge in that it has been leaking water after rainfall so I've got the Caterer and Handyman together so that we can investigate the situation and look for remedies.

Firstly, we went into the walk-in fridge so the Caterer could show us where the roof was leaking.

After we've done that, we start to make our way outside to have a look at it from the other angle. As we exit the kitchen via the rear door, the Caterer makes comment about the smell of burning and that someone has a fire on the go.

As we turn the corner to examine the fridge, there's an ashtray on the wall of the clubhouse and it's on fire!!

Before seeing us, the Caterer had been out for a cigarette and had clearly not ensured that it was fully extinguished!

Tuesday 19th February 2019

I know it goes against the grain with most golf club members that non-members are allowed to use the clubhouse, but nevertheless, most clubs are looking to maximise use of the facilities to generate additional income in order to balance the books. The club I was at was no different.

At lunchtime today, an elderly couple came into the clubhouse with their daughter who must have been in her late fifties herself. The gentleman was walking very unsteadily and was using a walker. He was passing the office and asked me if I could point him in the right direction for the toilets. Rather than give him directions verbally, I got up and asked him to follow me. I held the door as he went through to the changing rooms and in there, I decided I would take him all the way through to the disabled toilet so that he didn't have to navigate the step to the urinals and cubicles.

Once we had arrived at the disabled toilet, I opened the door, put the light on and told him I would wait outside so that I could ensure his smooth return to the lounge.

When he had finished, he opened the door and I joined him for the return journey. However, before proceeding, he uttered those immortal words "Can you zip me up please?"

Now I'm not going to lie, the first thoughts running through my mind were "I don't get paid enough to do that!" However, in the interest of customer services (!), I bent down to zip up his flies when he uttered the even more immortal words "Not there, my coat!!!"

Oops!!

Fortunately, no one witnessed this event, and he was fine to the point that once I had re-united him with his wife and daughter, he shook my hand for my assistance.

Thursday 21st February 2019

Last night was the monthly meeting of Council and I'd had been urging the President and the Captain to get the meeting over and done with as quickly as possible as I had arranged to have dinner afterwards with a friend who is over from France.

The Captain asks what her name is and I explain that my friend is a gay male, previously from Nottingham but now living in the South of France.

This morning, I receive an email from the Captain asking how my gay night went.

My response "Give us a kiss and I'll tell you!"

I heard no more about the subject from him!

Wednesday 27th February 2019

I have to visit the Professional's Shop to arrange providing our Handyman with two new polo shirts to work in. Whilst there, I notice that on display as part of a promotional campaign, they have one golf shoe that replicates that of Michael Jordan i.e. size 22!

One of the lady members had been heard to comment "If that is the size if his feet, what must be the size of his manhood!!!"

Her exact words have not been repeated here but I think you can guess!!

Tuesday 12th March 2019

There was more than a little trepidation in my journey to work today.

Yesterday, word had spread that travellers were in the area and potentially, identifying new 'camp sites'.

On arrival, the car park was clear! Phew!

Friday 22nd March 2019

I've got a big birthday coming up on Monday and as I'm having the day off to celebrate with a game of golf with my eldest son, I decided to have some new spikes put in my golf shoes.

I took them in yesterday and the Professional did them for me (together with giving them a clean!) and had put them back on my desk after I had left for the day.

I've been to his shop this morning to settle up with him and he told me that it was on him and that I should consider it my birthday present.

I told him that if he was better looking, I'd give him a kiss!

Friday 22nd March 2019

Two weeks ago, one of our staff left to embark in a new career as a self-employed landscape gardener and whilst we were very disappointed to lose him, obviously you can't stand in the way of people's ambitions.

He rang me this afternoon to say that he's not been paid today.

I tell him that we have this archaic system where if he has stopped working for us, then we've stopped paying him!!

Simples!

Monday 25th March 2019

I mentioned last year that 25th March is my birthday and this year is a BIG birthday so I've taken the day off to play golf with my eldest son at Wellingborough Golf Club.

Tuesday 2nd April 2019

It's the Grand National on Saturday on we have a member that organises a sweepstake on it each year.

He's been into the office today for help in getting it organised and we were very quick to remind him that when he came to get last year's organised, he'd actually got the information relating to the 2017 event and not the 2018 race!! I'm not a big follower of racing but did spot that some of the runners he had down weren't actually running.

I asked if he had Red Rum in the field and if so, could I have him!

Monday 8th April 2019

One of the issues we've had since the appointment of the new catering regime is the division of tips between kitchen staff, waiting on staff and the bar staff, the issue being that the bar staff having been getting any!

This had been ongoing for some time and whilst, I had been continually led to believe that the matter had been resolved, it clearly hadn't to the point where I received a stern word from the President. As a result, I wrote a procedure to be followed which was agreed by catering and bar staff and was put into practice a few weeks ago and it had been running smoothly.

On Monday mornings, my role is to count the tips that are held in a secure tin (there's only me that has a key) and then divide it up between those that worked. This is calculated from the hours on timesheets produced by the caterer and bar.

So far, so good.

Today, I've counted the tips and got the timesheet from the bar but as I'm waiting for the sheet from catering, I went in search. The Caterer is not in today but his No.2 is and I explain that I need the information as to who worked and leave it with him.

Shortly after, he brings the information but 'on the back of a fag packet'. Not strictly 'on the back of a fag pack' – my terminology – but on a scrap piece of paper.

I showed him a copy of the agreed procedure, which states that their timesheet should be produced, and he explained that he didn't bring that to me in case I lost it!!

I explained to him that;-

    a. The only people that lose things around here are the caterers and

    b. The lost thing I lost was my virginity!!!

Friday 16th April 2019

Some while ago, the Head Greenkeeper had this wonderful idea to set up a 'WhatsApp' group as a communication tool between his team, the staff in the Professional's Shop and myself. This meant that we would all be copied in on course information so we all knew what was going on.

I'm not in today as its Good Friday but I've received a message from the Professional as part of this group saying that a member has just reported to him that on the thirteenth hole, there's no flag or hole!!

Member's expectations?! It's a Bank Holiday! And that means there's a reduced service!!

Epilogue

A couple more 'stories' to relate before closing.

Here's one relating to a disciplinary issue at a club. I'm not going to mention which one as it's not really relevant but I'm sure you'll find it as amusing as I did.

Having spent a week here now and seen the amount of paper being needlessly retained, I've decided to have a look through a filing cabinet to see what information needs to be retained and what can be disposed of.

Amongst the files held in that cabinet is the Disciplinary File and nothing beats a good read of its contents.

One of the files contains details of an incident in the clubhouse following a social event at the club and the read left me in stitches. The best way to recall this incident is to provide two statements word for word in relation to the incident.

The first is from the Bar Staff that was on duty at the time;-

On the date in question, I was working the evening function for a member's private party. Everything was going fine until after bar closing when I started to politely ask people to start drinking up. This was done at 12.30am. By 12.45am, no progress had been made so I started asking again, this time adding can you start drinking up and making your way out so I can lock and secure the premises. All agreed except for one person who dismissed my comment. I could tell from her response that she was going to be a problem. Everyone except for that person and her company made their way out to awaiting taxis. I was told by her to give her five minutes which she then walked over to her friend to say something. I never heard what was said but I could tell by her friend's expression that she was shocked by the comments made. I then asked her if she had a coat in the locker room and if not, I was going to lock and secure it, which she responded that she was trying to drink her drink in memory of what she told me was her dead dad. I said that I was sorry to hear about her dead dad but does she have a coat to collect from the locker room. She then responded with an angry tone and said five minutes and yes she did have a coat and a big with her house keys which she needed so I couldn't lock them up as she had left kids home alone and I can't leave them home alone all night. I then stood back with another member of staff as I was shocked by her comments and decided to give her some space as I didn't want her to get aggressive. The time was now 1.00am and she decided that it was time to collect her coat, her bag, do her hair, makeup and go to the toilet. All said in a sarcastic tone implying that I would have to wait until she had done all of that. I ignored the comment and went behind the bar to away the till drawers and to check with my co-worker what else needed to be done. I then collected the keys from the back and proceeded with my colleague to lock the Gents which we did and went out the back door to come through the back door of the Ladies hoping that by that time, she would have made her way out. As we made our way towards the ladies front locker room door with me following, she was standing by the door chatting away. She opened the door and *told us to go first which I thought was a polite gesture. But no sooner had I walked through the door she said "Now leave as I am talking" and went to slam the door in my face which I was shocked and found very rude, but as my foot was in the door as I held it open after I walked through she couldn't do so. I still politely at this point said that it was well after closing and that she would need to leave the premises so I could lock and secure it. She did walk through but got to the double glass doors and shouted you fucking little bitch. Which I found highly unnecessary as I had done nothing wrong. The time was now about 1.06am. I locked the Ladies door and me and my colleague walked towards the front door to lock it behind them. I was greeted by her in the foyer and hurled abuse and I told her that I was not going to tolerate that and she now needed to leave. She wouldn't have been waiting in the cold as the taxi had been there since 1.00am. She went to leave with her friend following but she turned quickly which from my assessment of the situation was to come at me but knocked her friend to the floor in the process. I alone helped her friend up with her still hurling abuse at me. All the time, her friend was asking her to shut up as she was making a fool of herself and her other half stood with an expressionless face as if was the norm is only how I can describe it. He didn't seem bothered by her actions at all. I told her to leave again or I'll call the police and her friend managed to pull her out of the door while her husband looked on and as she shouted I'm going to do you for assault as you hit me. By this point, I had had enough and she came back through the door so I proceeded, scared with what she might do to call the police. I called the police but they never showed up until 1.30am which by that time she had left in her taxi. But she did sit and wait in the taxi for at least five minutes with how it would seem waiting for me. The whole situation put me into shock that my whole body shook as I wasn't expecting her to make such a big deal of the situation. I couldn't leave the golf club until I stopped shaking as I couldn't drive like that so didn't leave the premises until gone 2.00am with my colleagues.*

So that's the statement of the member of the Bar Staff and here's the statement from the person with whom she was having that altercation;-

<u>*To whom it may concern*</u>

On the evening in question, I was at a Christmas Party which I have attended for three years now. I had a wonderful Christmas dinner, food and company I cannot complain. I then went on the dance floor, as I am devoted to dancing I did not stop until the disco had finished. We were going to a friend's house for further drinks and I was in a excited, happy mood. All my friends were around me and I was buzzing with happiness. I have some good friends in the village and have done a lot for charity in the last seven years and I am very highly thought of. As soon as I picked up my drink and involved myself in conversations and laughter, the bar staff was in my face, as close as twelve inches. I found her to be invading my space as she told me to drink up now. She said this in a rude, disrespected manner as to I was taken aback by her tone. I told her I was finishing my drink as someone had just bought it for me and I wanted to drink it to my late father in law. Her answer to this was to take the glass outside. When I replied and told her is that alright, she said that she did not care. I felt individually attacked as there were about twelve people there at this stage and none of them were spoken to at all. Never mind in this manner. Shortly, after that we were all still laughing and enjoying ourselves as we did not see the seriousness of what was happening when she told myself and to which someone overheard, I was to get my belongings and I had sixty seconds to do so or the changing room door was being locked. My children were at home and the keys were in my bag, when I mentioned this to her, she said it is not her problem. I have a son with a heart defect and has undergone major operations and I did not expect that response. Three of us went in the changing room to get our belongings and go to the toilet as we were walking home. She was waiting with a rude, angry expression at the door as we walked out. We made our way to the door to leave when she said that she was going to call the police. We were leaving so there was no need for that. At that stage, she grabbed my arm and pushed me. I reacted and went back at her and in the process, knocked my best friend over. She got up and left. In the other statement, she wrote that my friend came back, she never. I think at that stage, she knew she had assaulted me and ran off crying. I feel that she panicked and thought "Oh God, what have I done?" I shouted through the door that she had assaulted me and I was going to inform the police. In my opinion, she spoke to me with disrespect, rudeness and in a manner that was not *appropriate. I was brought up to use manners and respect for my elders. I have been told this apparently in the world we live in today. I have brought my children up with the same morals I had. If I thought my children were talking to people like that I would be annoyed and ashamed. I will not tolerate anyone speaking to me like that. I am so annoyed that she has thrown this out of all proportion. I feel that because she assaulted me, she has panicked and made all these allegations such as I had a taxi waiting for me since 1.00am and I sat in the taxi for five minutes waiting for her. If there was a taxi there, why didn't she take the taxi name and number and when the police attended later, surely they could have investigated it. I have a number of people that can clarify that I walked home that night. I am also annoyed to her reaction to my children were home alone. My eldest is fifteen years old. This is no business of hers. Also saying my so called husband looked on with an expressionless face as if was the norm. I found this very upsetting and offensive, she has no right to say these things about my husband. The final reason is there is so much gossip going around the village that I punched her and club members saying untruthful things. I feel this is confidential and to not expect my name to be slandered which I will take further as well. I have informed the police and will be taking the assault further if I do not get an apology from her. And I think you should think long and hard whether to employ someone who speaks to paying members like that and obviously tries to cause trouble. As I have heard it's not the first time. Would she speak to a group of men in that manner? Or would she tell a disabled person they had sixty seconds to get their belongings? I feel that I was individually picked on that night for what reason I am trying to find out but as I said earlier, it has been blown out of proportion and none of it was necessary. I hope to hear from you in due course with an apology.*

Unfortunately, I cannot report the outcome of this matter, but I think that it is incidental to the content of these two statements!

And finally………..

I have mentioned earlier in the book that my birthday is on 25th March and that in 2019, I celebrated a BIG birthday and to make the most of it, I decided to visit the U.S. Open being held in June of that year at Pebble Beach, California.

Before getting there, I'd visited San Francisco, Los Angeles, the Grand Canyon, Las Vegas before arriving at Pebble Beach for the weekend's play on Saturday 15th June.

What a wonderful place! What a wonderful experience!

Just the U.S, PGA Championship and the Masters to go now to complete my Grand Slam!!

That then rounds off my first ten years in golf club management.

I hope you have enjoyed the read and now understand that the job is **NOT ALL ABOUT GOLF!!**